Aromas Of Sindh

100 RECIPES FROM THE HEART

Aromas Of Sindh

100 RECIPES FROM THE HEART

A collection of one hundred sweet and savory vegetarian
recipes and tales from the author's truly Sindhi upbringing

GEETA GWALANI

BLACK EAGLE BOOKS
2020

BLACK EAGLE BOOKS

USA address:
7464 Wisdom Lane
Dublin, OH 43016

India address:
E/312, Trident Galaxy, Kalinga Nagar,
Bhubaneswar-751003, Odisha, India

E-mail: info@blackeaglebooks.org
Website: www.blackeaglebooks.org

First International Edition Published by
BLACK EAGLE BOOKS, 2020

Aromas of Sindh: 100 recipes from the heart!

by **Geeta Gwalani**

Cover & Interior Design: Pathrika by Mekala

ISBN- 978-1-64560-123-4. (Paperback)
ISBN- 978-1-64560-124-1. (Hardcover)
ISBN- 978-1-64560-125-8. (Ebook)
Library of Congress Control Number: 2020947945

Printed in United States of America

This book of my favorite Sindhi recipes is dedicated to my dearest Mother -- an entrepreneur, an artist and a home-maker; who in her short life achieved so much and from whose life I inherited a great sense of both fashion and interior design! To my Father, to whom I owe everything I am professionally and personally – who taught me to give my best at what I do, be persistent, principled and disciplined; who taught me to live a healthy and happy life.

To my sister, who is a successful surgeon, and my role model and to my brother who is the true inspiration in my life.

I am also ever so grateful for the support I received from my husband; for trying all of the 100 and more recipes that I made and encouraging me along the way…

As I started putting this book together, I thought I would barely remember 30 or 40 dishes, but the Sindhi cuisine abounds in options…I have not even included the famous Sindhi Teevarn (Mutton) or Pallo (Pomfret) and other meat dishes! I have not included the multiple Papad or Kheecha recipes that we savored as kids. I save those for the next version!

For all, which I remember of the Sindhi cuisine, I have my childhood experiences to thank and each time I wrote something about a recipe, there would be a smile on my face, a twinkle in the eye and sometimes a tear. But, there would always be my mom's smiling face, who found time, amongst all her many artistic and design endeavors, to make fresh meals and snacks for all of us. I also remember by grandmother who would help her from time to time especially when they made Papad!

I am indebted to my father who taught us to read and write our beautiful language, Sindhi. When he started teaching us the Sindhi alphabet we were so upset that we had to learn a language of which we would use nothing at school, but now I think of it as

my most valuable possession. I am proud that today, we are among the few that can read and write this language.

I am thankful that our childhood was filled with laughter, love, and aromas of our wonderful cuisine. This book has been a learning experience for me too. There are recipes that I had forgotten but thanks to the internet these took me back in time…I am thankful for the resources we have now.

In a very big part, this book is a tribute to the indomitable spirit of the Sindhis, who have, in the face of many hardships, been successful, prosperous and generous.

Lastly but not the least, I am thankful for the critiques from my family and friends and most of all from the person who has helped in designing this book. She pushed me to take better and better pictures and do justice to each and every element of the dish.

I am grateful that the book has turned out to be beautiful and charming in a very unique way. I have in my pictures, tried to have an element or two of my loved ones. My mom's saree, my dad's book, their favorite Sindhi newspaper – 'Hindwasi', the many scarves and sarees that my sister and brother have gifted me…all find place in this book.

"Aromas of Sindh" is my miniscule contribution to the rich heritage of the world's oldest culture from Indus Valley. Each recipe is from the heart, desirous of preserving and furthering our cuisine and our culture across the globe.

As chef and gourmand, I am amazed at the culinary possibilitie the world over and how food has this unique quality to brin, together different cultures and its people. Having lived an worked in so many continents, I have had the joy and pleasure c both, learning and sharing my own food journeys.

But Indian food and the numerous micro-cuisines it represent will always stay close to my heart; especially when it is from m own homeland – Sindh.

'Aromas of Sindh' is a beautiful collection of over 100 vegetaria recipes. While many of our recipes are well known, some of ou preparations have been forgotten and it is indeed wonderful tha more than a 100 recipes have been prepared and put together i a single book.

I am also delighted to be writing the foreword for a cookboo compiled by a fellow Sindhi who has been able to documen what she learnt from her mother and present it in a very aestheti way. It is true that nothing compares to a simple meal prepared by a mother for her family and even the simplest dishes becom flavorful because they are made from the heart!

I believe this book and our cuisine is a great way to keep us al bound to our culture in some form and also pass it on for generation to come.

With pride, I present to you, '**Aromas of Sindh – A 100 recipe from the heart**'.

Chef Vicky Ratnani

Index

Breakfast

Sindhi breakfast is what breakfast food should be! Healthy, yet rich and filling! Mostly dominated by flours – wheat and Jowar, dairy - yoghurt and homemade white butter and the occasional Dal Pakwan, Seyal Manyun ain Bread and Sayoon Patata our breakfast spread is definitely flavorful tingling both the sweet and the savory taste buds!

The healthy Kokyun, Lola, Phulka, Bhatt, Dodha have been a source of nutrition and loving conversations…

KOKI (BASAR WARI)
(Wheat flat bread with onions)

In many ways, I think Sindhis and their cuisine belong to the world. The original seafarers, businesspersons, and entrepreneurs – we have made the world our home, country, state!

So I think because they travelled so much, they must have had to have something staple that would last at least a couple of days and I think KOKI was born as a result!

Just my theory and I say this because we would find Basar (Onion) Wari Koki often in our school lunch box and I would often wonder whether it was Mom's magic that made the bread taste so heavenly even while it was not warm.

Baba (my Father) would always eat it with a small bowl of yoghurt and some yellow or white butter melting on it while it was warm. Me, sometimes I have eaten it like a full meal complete with home made butter, yoghurt and tea. Other times I have dashed out of home in the mornings with Koki in hand while leaving for work. It works for me...this 'transformational' ability of this simple food…

So here's the run down on this healthy, yet yummy traditional Sindhi breakfast. (Of course you can also eat it at Lunch, snack and dinner). Loved by all with a dollop of yoghurt and Sindhi Papad.

ONE

Koki

30 MINS   3 PIECES   MEDIUM

INGREDIENTS

Wheat Flour – 1 cup

Onion – ¼ cup (finely chopped)

Green Chilies – as per taste (finely chopped)

Salt – as per taste

Water – as required

Cooking Oil – 1 tbsp for the dough and then some for roasting the Koki

Step 1: Mix all the ingredients. Knead into a medium stiff dough using small quantities of water.

Step 2: Next heat the griddle and make small flat balls. Roast them lightly on the griddle such that both sides are partially cooked.

Step 3: Next roll these again and place them on the hot griddle. Cook each side, on medium flame, drizzling little oil till each side is a beautiful golden brown.

Serve warm with yoghurt, pickle, tea and papad. Koki stays fresh for at least a couple of days so it is ideal for long work days or play days for kids.

SEYAL PHULKO/ SEYAL MANI
(Cooked Bread)

This is a mouthwatering, simply delicious snack and you will know why once you make it. What makes it special is that this recipe has my mother's signature since it follows a slightly different style than usual. Garlic is the queen of this dish!

We love Seyal Phulko as breakfast and as snack at tea-time too. Essentially, this dish is made from left over phulka (Indian wheat bread) that are often used over the following morning making it a very desirable breakfast.

This recipe takes me back to my childhood days when we would love to pick the garlicky triangular pieces of phulka directly from the pan (kadhai), the three of us giggling away at our own jokes and playing with abandon till mom found out that we were smuggling all the food!!!

TWO

Seyal Phulko

⏱ 15 MINS   🍴 SERVES 2   👨‍🍳 EASY

INGREDIENTS

Left over Phulka/ Rotis (Indian wheat bread) – 2

Garlic – 10 to 12 cloves

Chilis – 2 to 3 (adjust as per taste)

Cumin Seeds – 1 tbsp

Fresh Coriander – ¼ cup (chopped)

Turmeric Powder – ¼ tsp

Salt – as per taste

Oil – 2 to 3 tbsps

Step 1: In a mortar-pestle grind the garlic (10-12 cloves), green chilis (as per taste) cumin seeds and fresh coriander into a semi-fine paste. Add some salt and turmeric powder.

Step 2: Take a small portion of this paste in a plate and add very little water. Take the phulka/rotis and cut into half. Now dip these in this garlic paste water for a minute or two.

Step 3: Next take the semi-fine garlic chili paste and layer it on each half of the phulko/roti and fold it such that it looks like a triangle. Make such stuffed triangles with all the phulka/rotis.

Step 4: Heat some oil in a pan and add cumin seeds and turmeric powder. Sauté for a few seconds and then place each stuffed triangular phulko/roti in the pan.

Step 5: Pour very little water and cook covered, on medium to low heat. Open the pan after 5-7 minutes, turn the side, add some water and cook covered.

When both sides are lightly browned, take them out and serve.

Serve hot with chutney or ketchup or just like that; they will taste divine!

SAYOON PATATA
(Sweet Vermicelli and Potatoes)

Sayoon Patata is a signature Sindhi breakfast. Pairing sweet with savory is probably not so common but here is one dish that balances the two beautifully! Sayoon – the sweet vermicelli and Patata – the savory and tangy potatoes!

I remember, as a child, I did not like the Vermicelli and would just eat the Potatoes, but this dish has grown on me and I long for this Sunday treat so often. My sister now often reminds and chides me that at one time, I did not quite fancy this dish and here I am now, waiting to make and eat this dish whenever I can!

THREE

Sayoon Patata

20 MINS   SERVES 3   EASY

INGREDIENTS

FOR SAYOON (VERMICELLI)

Vermicelli – 1 cup (use the fine variety)

Ghee – 1 tbsp

Sugar – ½ cup (adjust as per taste)

Water – ½ to ¾ cup

Green Cardamom – 3 to 4

Almond Slivers – for garnish

FOR PATATA (POTATOES)

Potatoes – 3 to 4 medium sized (peeled and chopped)

Cumin Seeds – ½ tsp

Chili Powder – ¼ tsp

Coriander Powder – ½ tsp

Turmeric Powder – ¼ tsp

Mango Powder – ¼ tsp

Salt – as per taste

SAYOON (Vermicelli)

Step 1: First, heat some ghee in a heavy-bottomed pan and then add the crushed green cardamoms. Roast the vermicelli on lowest flame until it turns a lovely golden color.

Step 2: Next, add the water and let the vermicelli cook in the water. You can now increase the flame to medium high.

Step 3: When the vermicelli is almost cooked, add the sugar and on low flame, let the vermicelli absorb the rest of the moisture and the added sugar.

Step 4: Once the water is all soaked in, switch off the flame, cover, and rest the vermicelli for at least 5 to 10 minutes before garnishing with almond slivers.

PATATA (Potatoes)

Step 1: Peel and chop the potatoes in small cubes. Heat oil in a pan and add cumin seeds.

Step 2: Next add the potatoes and all the dry spices – turmeric powder, chili powder, coriander powder, mango powder and salt to taste.

Step 3: Cover and cook until the potatoes are done.

Serve Sayoon and Patata warm at breakfast. You will love this unique combination!

MITHO LOLO
(Sweet Wheat Bread)

Mitho Lolo is a Thadri preparation. Thadri (Thad means cold) is a Sindhi festival that is a day dedicated to Shitala Devi, one who is believed to cure 'Mata' or Poxes. On this day the stove is not lit and hence no meal is cooked on the day. All the preparations are done the day before, prayers are offered to the stove and a few drops of water are sprinkled on it.

Since food is not cooked on the day of Thadri, Lolo, Koki, Besani and dry vegetables such as potato, okra or bitter gourd (karela), Matho (savoury buttermilk with boondi) are prepared the day before.

Ours was a joint family and I remember that my mother and grandmothers would make all the preparations the day before and store the Lolos and Besani in a Stainless Steel box wrapped in a cloth. The next morning the lolos would be served with homemade white butter and Matho.

We loved the Lolos that my mom would make and we would often be taking bites all through the day of this delicious food. Combined with homemade white butter this made for the most 'sinful' of all foods!

FOUR

Mitho Lolo

25 MINS   4 PIECES   EASY

INGREDIENTS

Wheat Flour – 2 cups

Sugar – ½ cup (soak in ¼ cup water for at least 2 hours so that it dissolves completely. You can also dissolve the sugar by boiling the water, strain and let it cool completely.)

Ghee (Clarified Butter) – 6 tbsp

Salt – a pinch

Cardamom Powder – ¼ tsp

Step 1: First lightly mix the ghee into the wheat flour and ensure that it is spread evenly. Next add the salt and cardamom powder.

Step 2: Now knead the flour with the sugar water pouring it little by little into a stiff dough.

Step 3: Next take a small portion and roll it into a thick round shaped bread. Make a couple of slits on the bread since it is thick, so that it cooks completely when roasted.

Step 4: Roast both sides on a girdle, on low flame, adding ghee on both sides till both sides have become golden brown.

Serve Mitho Lolo warm or cold with white butter or yoghurt.

CHEHRO PHULKO
(Savory Wheat Bread)

This is a very commonly eaten breakfast/lunch especially when there is no time to make anything else or when there are no other breakfast items or even vegetables.

We ate 'Chehro Phulko' with homemade yoghurt and Papad relishing the savory taste with each bite.

FIVE

Chehro Phulko

25 MINS   SERVES 4   MEDIUM

INGREDIENTS

Wheat Flour – 1 cup

Water – to knead dough

Oil – 1 tsp for kneading the dough and more while roasting the phulko

Salt – as per taste

Red Chili Powder – ½ tsp

Step 1: In a vessel/plate, knead a soft dough using wheat flour and water. Pour water a little at a time when kneading and once the dough comes together, apply some oil. Knead for a few more minutes so that it stays soft.

Step 2: Cover and rest for 10 minutes. The dough should be soft and pliable and should not stick to your fingers.

Step 3: Take a small portion, roll into a roundel, then dust with wheat flour, and using a rolling pin, roll into a small round phulko/roti.

Step 4: Next apply some oil using a brush or with your fingers. Then spread a little salt and chili powder all over the small phulko/roti.

Step 5: Then fold this small phulko into a roundel, dust with wheat flour and now using the rolling pin, roll into the normal phulko/roti i.e. about 6 – 8 inches in diameter.

Step 6: Roast on a girdle on medium flame and turn the sides of the Phulko. Drizzle oil when almost done and roast until both sides turn golden brown.

Serve hot with yoghurt and papad!

BHATT
(Cracked Wheat Sweet Porridge)

Our growing up years were full of healthy, homemade meals and 'Bhatt' was an integral part of our cuisine. Full of nutrients, sweetened with jaggery, this was a perfect breakfast.

My mom made 'bhatt' often for us since it is so easy to make and besides we now know that it is a natural source of B-vitamins, minerals, fibre and protein! Especially if we were recovering from a fever, she would insist that we eat Bhatt so that we could feel better soon and then be able to play with our friends!

I made Bhatt often when my son was little; as a baby, he would smack his lips and ask for more. But as his taste continues to change, I make Bhatt more often for myself and request him to have a spoon or two!

Very healthy and made with everyday ingredients, serve Bhatt to your loved ones especially the little ones!

SIX

Bhatt

20 MINS   SERVES 2   EASY

INGREDIENTS

Cracked Wheat (Bulgar Wheat/ Dalia/Lapsi) – ½ cup

Ghee – 2 tbsps

Jaggery – 4 tbsps

Cardamom Powder – ¼ tsp

Almond Slivers – for garnish

Raisins (optional) – 8 to 10

Water – 2.5 cups

Step 1: In a pan, (you could also use a pressure cooker if the cracked wheat is not the fine variety), on low flame, heat the ghee and roast the cracked/bulgar wheat until it is a nice golden brown.

Step 2: Add water (quantity would increase depending on the cracked wheat. I have used the fine variety in my recipe), cardamom powder and raisins (if using) and cook the cracked wheat. When the wheat is almost cooked, add in the Jaggery (you could adjust the amount as desired). Cook until the wheat is soft and ready to eat. The consistency of bhatt is like a porridge. You could increase the water quantity depending on the consistency preferred.

If using a pressure cooker, cook the wheat for about 2 to 3 whistles.

Step 3: Remove the 'bhatt' in a serving bowl and garnish with almond slivers.

Many recipes use milk instead of water, but this is the traditional Sindhi style 'bhatt'. You could also make it savory like 'upma' with vegetables.

Serve this healthy dish warm at breakfast time or whenever you are hungry!

DAL PAKWAN
(Yellow Lentils with flaky, crunchy bread)

Here's a Sindhi delicacy that appeals to the young and old alike. This lip-smacking dish has stayed at favorite position for generations, at our parties, social gatherings and general Sindhi festive lunches!

And I am so happy and grateful that this recipe has been passed down to me by my family …in fact this dish has been such an integral part of our household that I have forgotten when I first made it!

I haven't forgotten though that it has always been loved and has pulled everyone together at the dinner table (especially the not-so-hungry ones!) gently nudging us to share stories of the day, while the dal melts in the mouth and the crispy pakwan makes crunchy noise even as we speak!!!

I am so delighted to pass on to you what I have received from my family and I hope that you will make it with the same measure of love that my mother used and that mothers across the world use!

Serve Dal Pakwan with Green coriander Chutney and Sweet Chutney (Dates, Tamarind and Jaggery) along with finely chopped onions and experience the magic of this culinary delight!

From me to you...

SEVEN

Dal Pakwan

25 MINS   SERVES 2   DIFFICULT

INGREDIENTS

DAL

Chana Dal (Bengal Gram Lentils) – 1 cup

Cumin Seeds – ½ tsp

Turmeric Powder – ½ tsp

Chili Powder – ½ tsp

Coriander Powder – ¾ tsp

Mango Powder – ½ tsp

Cumin Powder – ¼ tsp

Oil – for cooking

PAKWAN

All Purpose Flour – 1 cup

Cumin Seeds – ½ tsp

Oil for dough – 1 tbsp

Salt – ½ tsp or as per taste

Oil – for deep frying

DAL

Step 1: Rinse and soak dal for about 3 hours.

Step 2: In a pressure cooker add the dal, salt and turmeric powder and 1.5 -2 cups of water and 'pressure cook' for about 2-3 whistles. Open the lid once it depressurizes naturally.

Step 3: Add water to adjust the consistency. Do not mash dal.

Step 4: Take the dal out in the serving bowl. With your fingers, sprinkle all the spices– red chili, coriander, cumin and mango powders – all over the dal.

Step 5: In a small pan, heat some oil. When the oil is hot, add the cumin seeds and when they crackle, immediately pour this hot oil over all the spice powders.

Your dal is ready.

PAKWAN

Step 1: Combine the flour, cumin seeds, salt and tablespoon of oil. Knead into medium stiff dough adding small quantities of water.

In the meanwhile heat enough oil in a frying pan.

Step 2: Next roll the dough and prick the pakwan with fork so that it does not fluff up when you fry.

Step 3: Fry on medium to low flame pressing the pakwan down so that it is crispy. Fry to a golden brown color on both sides.

Dal Pakwan is served with Pakwan in room temperature and the Dal piping hot.

Serve pakwan with dal garnished with finely chopped onions and coriander, sweet chutney and green chutney, pickle and papad.

CHAIN KOKI (KARAN MIRCHAN WARI)
(Wheat Flatbread with black pepper and Tea)

This Koki is made during winters and eaten at breakfast along with Cardamom Tea. That is exactly how I remember this preparation - the aroma of Elaichi (Cardamom) and the sizzling of oil while roasting the Koki.

As kids we loved this breakfast because we were allowed to dip the Koki in small cups of the sweet tea. We loved the taste of the cardamom flavored sweet tea, which my mom served in an old-fashioned steel kettle.

We were not otherwise allowed to drink tea as kids but with this Koki mom made an exception. And in those cold wintry mornings the black peppered Koki and warm tea made a very very hearty combination.

Even today, I make this recipe exactly as Mom would make it and only wish that it would taste as good as hers.

EIGHT

Chain Koki

30 MINS   3 PIECES   MEDIUM

INGREDIENTS

Wheat Flour – 1 cup

Crushed Black Pepper – 1 tsp

Cumin Seeds – 1 tsp

Cooking Oil – 1 tbsp for the dough and then some for lining the Koki

Water – as required

Step 1: In a vessel, mix the flour, crushed black pepper and cumin seeds. Add the oil well and mix with your fingers so that the flour resembles breadcrumbs. Knead into a medium stiff dough using small quantities of water.

Step 2: Next heat the griddle and make small flat balls. Roast them lightly on the griddle such that both sides are partially cooked.

Step 3: Next roll these again into about 7" discs and place them on the hot griddle. Drizzle oil on each side and roast on medium flame, until each side is a beautiful golden brown.

Serve this Koki warm with Cardamom Tea. You can also serve this with Dal Moong, the recipe of which, is in this book.

GUD JO PHULKO/ BUSRI
(Jaggery stuffed flatbread)

Gud jo Phulko is a healthy breakfast that I remember having so often

My mother would make this for the three of us and just one each would be enough. We could go through the entire day without eating- it was that filling! My father loved it too and he would love to eat with us and serve us a spoonful more of that yummy smooth homemade white butter! How our parents pamper us!

Made with homemade ghee, topped with homemade white butter and stuffed with jaggery! Just the thought of it makes me drool! Of course, it was ideal for winters and our little tummies would be satiated with the warmth of all the love and the jaggery too!

My son loves Gud jo Phulko. I make it for him often in the winters and both of us eat this just like my father would eat with me, me reminiscing those times with my Dad and my son telling me his stories of the day!

NINE

Gud jo Phulko

30 MINS   2 PIECES   EASY

INGREDIENTS

Wheat Flour – 1 cup

Water – as required

Jaggery – 1 tbsp for each phulko

Ghee – 1 tsp for each phulko

White Butter (yellow will do fine too) – a dollop!

Step 1: In a vessel, combine wheat flour and water and make a semi-soft dough just like the dough used to make Phulko/Roti.

Step 2: With a rolling pin, roll two Phulkas. Take one Phulko and sprinkle jaggery pieces all around the phulko except the edges. Apply ghee on the edges.

Step 3: Now place the second Phulko on top and seal the edges pressing down with your fingers, sealing the jaggery between the two Phulkas.

Step 4: Heat a griddle on medium flame. Lower the flame and put this phulko on it. Roast each side increasing the flame to medium for some time.

Step 5: Drizzle ghee all around it and roast until both the sides turn golden brown.

Step 6: Serve when hot because the jaggery would have melted. Open the seal and add a dollop of butter inside and outside!

Enjoy this delicious treat with your family!

This one is a winter breakfast winner!

BESANI
(Gram Flour Flatbread)

Besani is made exactly like the Basar Wari Koki except that you replace the wheat flour with Besan (gram flour). And typically also add some crushed Anardana (dried Pomegranate seeds), Ajwain (carom Seeds) and very little Kasuri Methi (Dry Fenugreek leaves).

The rest of the preparation is the same as the Basar Wari Koki.

Besani is one of the many preparations of bread eaten during Thadri festival on which day we do not light the stove. Some also call it Chehro Lolo (Savoury Bread).

TEN

Besani

⏱ 30 MINS 🍽 3 PIECES 👨‍🍳 MEDIUM

INGREDIENTS

Gram Flour – 1 cup

Onion – ¼ cup (finely chopped)

Green Chili – 1 (finely chopped)

Dried Pomegranate Seeds – ¼ tsp

Carom Seeds – ¼ tsp

Dry Fenugreek Leaves – ¼ tsp

Coriander Leaves – ¼ cup (finely chopped)

Salt – as per taste

Water – as required

Cooking Oil – 1 tbsp for the dough and then some for roasting the Koki

Step 1: In a vessel, mix the gram flour along with the onions and all the other ingredients except the water. Mix well. Knead into a medium stiff dough using small quantities of water.

Step 2: Next heat the griddle and make small flat balls. Roast them lightly on the griddle such that both sides are partially cooked.

Step 3: Next roll these again into about 7" discs and place them on the hot griddle. Drizzle oil on each side and roast on medium flame, until each side is a beautiful golden brown.

Serve Besani warm or at room temperature with Yoghurt, pickle or Papad. Or it can be eaten just like that too!

JUAR JO DHODHO
(Sorghum Millet flour savory Flatbread)

Dhodho is a flatbread and can be made with a variety of millets – Juar or Jowar or Sorghum Millet, Ragi or Nachni or Finger Millet or Bajri or Bajra or Pearl Millet.

Traditionally Sindhis prefer Juar jo Dhodho but I remember that my father loved Ragi jo Dhodho too because of its very high nutritional value. And Bajri jo Dhodho was often made as well. Probably because my parents had lived for a few years in Gadhinglaj, Kolhapur in Maharashtra where Bhakri made from Nachni or Bajra is a staple food. And so these millets too got incorporated in our cuisine.

Each month we used to get these millets individually ground at our neighborhood 'Chakki' place (flour mill). My parents, both loved dhodho with homemade white butter or yoghurt. A favorite breakfast item, I think these taste best when warm.

Nowadays, I also make sweet laddoos (Indian sweets) using Juar and these turn out delicious. But lets get back to Dhodho – this delightful and healthy breakfast treat!

ELEVEN

Juar jo Dhodho

🕐 30 MINS   🍽 4 PIECES   👨‍🍳 MEDIUM

INGREDIENTS

Juar (Sorghum Millet) Flour – 1 cup

Onion – 1 small (finely chopped)

Green Chili – 1 or 2 (finely chopped)

Salt – as per taste

Coriander Leaves – ¼ cup (finely chopped)

Water – to knead the dough

Oil – to drizzle on the Dhodho (Flatbread)

Step 1: In a vessel, first combine the Juar flour, onion, chilis, coriander and salt. Using warm water, slowly make a soft dough.

Step 2: Heat a griddle on low flame. Now take a portion of the dough in your hands and flatten it, next place it on the griddle and slowly, by using your fingers keep spreading and flattening the dough on the griddle itself.

Step 3: Alternatively, on your kitchen table, you could also flatten it with your fingers on a baking or plastic sheet and then place it on the griddle.

Traditionally, the rolling pin is not used to roll the dough while making dhodho but you could if that works better.

Step 4: Once the dhodho is on the griddle and ready to be roasted, make a few slits with a knife (take care not to cut through the dhodho) so that it cooks through.

Step 5: Now on slow flame roast the dhodho, flipping the sides only when required. Dhodho can be brittle so be careful when flipping the side; try and do it only twice (once on each side).

Step 6: Next drizzle some oil, especially along the slits and roast till the dhodho is done.

Serve Dhodho warm at breakfast with homemade white butter and or yoghurt.

DAL JO PHULKO
(Lentils-stuffed wheat bread)

Stuffed parathas (Stuffed wheat bread) are a very simple and lovable way of feeding kids all the nutritious veggies, lentils and soy that they would normally turn their face away from. Dal Jo Phulko is, I think, one of those inventions of a mother! Filled with nutrients in every bite. Combined with yoghurt or butter, this makes for one very fulfilling and nourishing meal fo a growing up child.

My mom made Dal jo Phulko ever so often and all of us including my father would love to eat this hot with Amul butter melting on it. She would make this with green moong dal (Green Lentils) and we would also find this in our lunch boxes or a weekend breakfast. The good thing about this paratha is that it tastes equally good when cold, but we enjoy this most with butter melting all over it!

TWELVE

Dal jo Phulko

45 MINS   SERVES 2   MEDIUM

INGREDIENTS

FOR WHEAT BREAD

Wheat Flour – 1 cup

Oil – ½ tsp

Salt – ¼ tsp

Water – to knead into semi-stiff dough

STUFFING

Boiled Moong Dal (Whole Green Gram Lentils) – 1 cup

Red Chili Powder – ½ tsp

Coriander Powder – 1 tsp

Mango Powder – ½ tsp

Salt – as per taste

Step 1: In a vessel, combine wheat flour and salt. Add water little by little and knead a soft and pliable dough. Cover and keep aside till you make the stuffing.

Step 2: In a pressure cooker boil the 'overnight soaked' green moong dal (Green Lentils). Boiling the dal is the most important and tricky part of this recipe. More water and you will not be able to use it as a stuffing in the paratha. So when boiling add water such that it only barely covers the dal and then pressure cook it for at least 6-7 whistles (the time it takes to cook depends on the dal; sometimes it may cook with lesser number of whistles). In any case, the water should be completely absorbed so that it is easy to use it as stuffing.

Step 3: Add the spices to the cooked dal – salt, chili powder, coriander powder and mango powder. You can add other spices of your choice (green chili, garlic etc), but these are what we traditionally use.

Step 4: Now take a portion of the dough and using a rolling pin, roll into a circular disc, the size as big as your palm. Spread some oil first using a brush or your fingers, then take a spoonful of the dal stuffing and place it in the center. Bring the edges together at the center and pinch them to seal the stuffing.

Step 5: Next, flatten this ball and dust both sides with wheat flour. Using the rolling pin, roll into a flat round shape. When rolling the ball, do it with a light hand and dust some more flour if required.

Step 6: Now you are ready to roast the phulko. On a heated griddle, on medium heat, place the Phulko and roast until both sides are almost done, flipping at regular intervals.

Step 7: When almost done, drizzle oil or ghee on both sides until they turn golden brown and are cooked through.

Serve warm with butter or yoghurt.

SEYAL BREAD/ SEYAL DABAL/ SEYAL PAV
(Cooked Bread)

Seyal Dabal like Seyal Phulko is a great snack or breakfast dish. At home, we usually made it for breakfast since it required basic ingredients and bread was readily available at our nearby 'Kirana' store.

This recipe is special because it uses the same unique style that my mother used for Seyal Phulko; the earthy garlic flavor blending in with the tomatoes and onions and making the bread full of flavor and even texture.

Eat this at tea time or breakfast, it is sure to tickle your taste buds and have you asking for some more.

THIRTEEN

Seyal Bread

30 MINS   SERVES 2   MEDIUM

INGREDIENTS

Bread – 4 slices (each slice cut into 4 pieces)

Garlic – 6 to 7 cloves

Green Chili – 1

Coriander Leaves – ½ cup

Water – as required

Onions – 1 medium (finely chopped)

Tomatoes – 1 medium (finely chopped)

Lemon Juice – for garnish

Red Chili Powder – ½ tsp

Turmeric Powder – ¼ tsp

Coriander Powder – ½ tsp

Oil – 1 tbsp

Salt – as per taste

Step 1: First make a garlic-coriander-chili paste in a mortal pestle. Take it out in a bowl (keep some aside) and add very little water and some salt.

Step 2: Now add the pieces of bread in this masala water, lightly coating all the pieces. Keep them soaked; the water should be absorbed completely, but the bread pieces do not turn mushy.

Step 3: In a heavy bottom pan, heat oil and sauté the onions on medium flame. Add in the saved garlic-coriander-chili paste.

Step 4: When the onions turn translucent, add the tomatoes and the spices – red chili, turmeric and coriander powders. Sauté on medium heat until the tomatoes turn mushy and the mixture releases oil.

Step 5: At this time, add very little water. Add some salt (there is salt in the paste so add accordingly).

Step 6: When this mixture comes to a boil, add the soaked bread pieces. Once the bread absorbs all the water and flavors, turn off the flame, sprinkle the lemon juice, and garnish with fresh coriander leaves.

Serve warm as breakfast or as your evening snack with tea.

HOLI JI ROAT/HOLI JO LOLO
(Holi's Wheat Flour Bread)

Holi- the festival of colors…I like this festival for the delicacies (Gheeyar, Pragree, Thaadal) and the pre-Holi events.

I especially remember that just before Holi, my grandfather or my mom would buy the dry cow dung cakes, which would be used to cook the wheat flour bread -'roat' (pronounced 'wrote')/Lolo.

We would follow a very traditional ritual on the evening before the Holi day. On a very large iron tray, my mom would light the dry cow dung cakes and cook the 'Roat' on them. (A cotton thread would be wrapped around the 'rot' / lolo five times forming a star (*). This would be symbolic of Lord Prahlad who did not burn though he was in the pyre with Holika.) Then fanning the hot cakes lightly with a paper, she would ensure that both sides of the 'Roat' were cooked evenly.

The following morning when the fire had cooled down, my mom would keep the iron tray at the small 'puja place' at home. Each of us in the family, would worship the ashes - taking a pinch and applying on our forehead, placing a flower, sprinkling gulal (red color) and also placing a small piece of sweet (mostly Gheeyar) and Roat on it. We would also eat the "roat"/lolo as Prasad (holy offering).

Today I make these Holi Rot/Lolo very often as breakfast because these are healthy and made with Jaggery and wheat flour. Of course, I make them on a griddle and serve them with a dollop of white butter.

Enjoy this very traditional bread, very easy to make and very healthy to eat!

Holi jo Lolo

⏱ 20 MINS   🍴 SERVES 2   👨‍🍳 MEDIUM

INGREDIENTS

FOR 2 ROAT/LOLO:

Wheat Flour – as required

Jaggery – 2 tbsp

Water – ¼ cup

Oil or Ghee – 1 tsp

Cardamom Powder – ¼ tsp

Ghee – to drizzle on the Roat/Lolo

Step 1: In a vessel, first, dissolve the jaggery in the water by keeping it in water for about 30 minutes. When it has dissolved, strain it and add a teaspoon of ghee and the cardamom powder.

Step 2: In this jaggery water, add wheat flour little by little and knead until a semi stiff dough is formed.

Step 3: Take a portion of the dough and with the rolling pin, roll into a small disc – about ½ inch in thickness and about 4 inches in diameter. Make small slits so that it is cooked well from the inside too.

Step 4: Roast this disc on a griddle on low flame. Drizzle some ghee once both sides are almost cooked.

Step 5: When both sides turn a nice golden brown, take it out and serve warm with some homemade butter.

Serve this healthy dish warm or at room temperature at breakfast or even lunch.

Main

Sindhi main course is dominated by the 'Seyal' style of preparation, which means cooking something in onion garlic base or onion tomato base with little or no water.

And then there is the other style, which uses only the dry spices and especially the Mango Powder or Ambachur. So many of the vegetable dishes are prepared by sautéing in oil and simply adding salt, coriander, turmeric and mango powders.

Of course the Sindhi style Sai Bhaji, Besan ji Bhaji and Kadhi are delightful but so are the bharyal karela and the many bhee (Lotus root) and dal preparations. And the very unusual Macroli Patata and Phoolpatasha add that slice of quirkiness to the Sindhi main course!

CHARAN JI DAL
(Bengal Gram Lentils)

Charan ji dal is a very commonly made dal in Sindhi households. We also use this dal when we make Dal Pakwan but when not making Pakwan, we make this dal differently and also eat it with Phulko or Bhuga Chanwar.

Almost all vegetables make a good side when eaten with this dal, but I remember that my mother would make both 'tikyun' (Aloo Tikki) and Bhuga Chanwar or she would make bheendi patata in the exact same style as Patata (in Sayoon Patata recipe) and Phulko.

What a delightful combination it would be!

I make Charan ji dal often especially at our lunch meal because it tastes good with any vegetable side and given the consistency of this preparation, it can be eaten with Phulko.

FIFTEEN

Charan ji Dal

30 MINS   SERVES 2   MEDIUM

INGREDIENTS

Bengal Gram – ½ cup

Onions – 1 medium sized (finely chopped)

Tomatoes – 1 medium sized (finely chopped)

Green Chili – 1 (finely chopped; increase the quantity if you want it more spicy)

Ginger-Garlic Paste – ½ tsp

Cumin Seeds – ¼ tsp

Turmeric Powder – ¼ tsp

Coriander Powder – ½ tsp

Garam Masala (optional) – ¼ tsp (for garnish)

Salt – as per taste

Coriander Leaves – for garnish (finely chopped)

Cooking Oil – 1 tbsp

Water – 1 cup

Step 1: Soak the lentils in water for at 3 to 4 hours or overnight. I a pressure cooker, heat the oil and add the cumin seeds. When the crackle add the onions, ginger-garlic paste and green chili. Sauté th mixture on medium heat.

Step 2: When onions turn light brown, add finely chopped tomatoes Let the mixture cook for some time and then add the spices – turmeri powder and coriander powder.

Step 3: When this mixture has cooked, leaves the sides and release oil, drain the water and add the soaked Bengal Gram Lentils. Let th lentils cook in the onion-tomato mixture for about 10 minutes on lov flame.

Step 4: Then add water and salt to taste. Close the lid of the pressur cooker and on high flame let the lentils cook for 3 to 4 whistles o until they are completely cooked.

Step 5: Open the cooker after it depressurizes naturally an adjust the consistency of the dal. Garnish with finely chopped fresl coriander leaves.

You can also sprinkle some Garam Masala, which is optional. usually don't, but I do sprinkle some freshly squeezed lemon juic – just a few drops for that tangy flavor!

MOONG DAL
(Small Yellow Lentils)

This is the recipe of the Moong dal that my mother would make every Monday dinner along with sanna pakora and Phulka.

Made with the Petite yellow lentils, this is very light and slightly more watery in consistency than our other lentil preparations.

Tastes great, both with Phulko and Chanwar (rice), enjoy this dal for a light, yet hearty meal along with yoghurt and pickle!

SIXTEEN

Moong Dal

⏱ 20 MINS   🍽 SERVES 2   👨‍🍳 EASY

INGREDIENTS

Moong Dal – ½ cup (washed and soaked for at least 30 mins)

Water – 1.5 cups

Tomatoes – 1 medium finely chopped

Dried Red Chili – 1 small

Cumin Seeds – ½ tsp

Curry Leaves – 5 to 6

Hing (Asoefetida) – a pinch

Turmeric Powder – ¼ tsp

Salt – as per taste

Coriander Leaves – for garnish (finely chopped)

Step 1: In a vessel, on medium flame, boil the lentils with wate. turmeric powder, tomatoes, and salt. Add some more water if it dries up.

Step 2: Once the lentils are cooked, whisk the lentils and add water to adjust consistency. Lower the flame and let the lentils simmer.

Step 3: Prepare the tempering by heating oil in a smaller pan and adding dried red chili, hing, curry leaves and cumin seeds in that order. When the cumin seeds crackle, pour the tempering over the lentils.

Give it a nice stir, cover and let the dal simmer for a few more minute before switching off the flame. Garnish with coriander leaves.

Serve with Phulko or Chanwar (Rice).

GUAR/ GWAR JI BHAJI
(Cluster Beans preparation)

Guar/Cluster Beans is a well-liked vegetable among the Sindhis. We add it in the Sindhi Kadhi and a side made with Guar and Patata, eaten with Phulko is also often prepared.

As kids, I remember we did not like this preparation but as grownups, we enjoy this bhaji and today I too make it very often.

Guar ji Bhaji

⏱ 25 MINS　　🍴 SERVES 3　　👨‍🍳 MEDIUM

INGREDIENTS

Guar/Gwar/Cluster Beans – 250 gms

Potato – 1 medium sized (peeled and diced into cubes)

Onions – 1 medium sized (finely chopped)

Tomatoes – 1 medium sized (finely chopped)

Ginger – t tsp grated

Garlic – 6 to 7 cloves crushed

Cumin Seeds – ½ tsp

Green Chili – 1 (finely chopped)

Turmeric Powder – ¼ tsp

Coriander Powder – ½ tsp

Roasted Cumin Powder – ¼ tsp

Red Chili Powder – ¼ tsp

Salt – as per taste

Water

Lemon Juice – 1 tsp

Coriander Leaves – for garnish (finely chopped)

Step 1: Wash the cluster beans; chop the top and the small tail like portion at the end. Then cut the cluster beans in 1 inch pieces. Peel and dice the potatoes into cubes.

Step 2: I make this dish in the pressure cooker. Heat oil on medium flame in the pressure cooker and add cumin seeds. When the cumin seeds crackle, add the finely chopped onions, grated ginger and crushed garlic.

Step 3: When onions turn a light golden brown, add the finely chopped tomatoes, green chili and the spices – turmeric, coriander, cumin and red chili powders. Sautee this onion tomato mixture until tomatoes turn mushy and the mixture releases oil and leaves the side of the cooker.

Step 4: Now add the chopped beans, potatoes and salt. Let the beans and potatoes cook for some time in this onion-tomato mixture on medium flame. Keep stirring.

Step 5: After the beans and potatoes have been in the mixture for some time, add two tablespoons of water, close the lid and pressure-cook the beans and potatoes on high flame for about 3 to 4 whistles. Switch off the flame.

Step 6: Open the lid of the pressure cooker only once it depressurizes naturally and check if the beans and potatoes are cooked. If they are cook the preparation on medium flame without the lid, to dry out any excess water.

Step 7: Before serving sprinkle lemon juice and garnish with fresh coriander leaves.

Eat Guar ji Bhaji at meal time with Phulko and a side of yoghurt.

SAYI DAL
(Split Green Lentils)

Sayi dal is a lentil preparation made from split green moong dal. It is yet another flavorful dal made often and served with phulko, a side of a bhaji (veggie) and yoghurt.

EIGHTEEN

Sayi Dal

⏱ 25 MINS   🍴 SERVES 2   👨‍🍳 EASY

INGREDIENTS

Split Green Lentils – ½ cup

Onions – 1 medium sized (finely chopped)

Tomatoes – 1 meidum sized (finely chopped)

Garlic – 3 to 4 cloves (crushed)

Green Chili – 1 (finely chopped)

Oil – 1 tbsp

Cumin Seeds – ½ tsp

Turmeric Powder – ¼ tsp

Coriander Powder – ½ tsp

Water – 1 cup or as required

Coriander Leaves – for garnish (finely chopped)

Step 1: Wash and soak the lentils for 15 to 20 minutes. In a pressure cooker on medium flame, heat oil and add cumin seeds. When the crackle, add the onions, green chili and garlic.

Step 2: Once the onions turn light golden brown, add the tomatoe and the spices- turmeric and coriander powders.

Step 3: Keep stirring the onion-tomato mixture until the tomatoes tur mushy and the mixture releases oil. At this point, add the wash and soaked lentils.

Step 4: Add water, close the lid and on high flame, cook the lentils fo 5 to 6 whistles or until the lentils are completely cooked.

Step 5: Open the lid when the cooker depressurizes naturally, whis the lentils, and garnish with finely chopped fresh coriander leaves You can add hot water to adjust its consistency.

Serve at meal time with Phulko or Chanwar and a side of yoghurt.

BHEE PATATA
(Lotus Root with Potatoes)

The Sindhi fascination with the lotus root is well known. Called 'Bhee' in Sindhi, this dish made with fresh lotus roots tastes fascinating. Bhee is used in a variety of ways in the Sindhi cuisine – Pakora (fritters), Tikki (Pattie) and even Chaat (savory snack).

But, Bhee patata is the favorite of all; it tastes good and is equally nutritious. My grandfather would bring these mud-laden roots wrapped in newspaper from the vegetable vendors and we would wonder how these 'sticks' could transform into the flavorful Bhee Patata.

The trick to making Bhee is the manner in which it is sliced. It absolutely must be sliced in a slant to avoid the hairy fibers of the Bhee getting in the way. My mother would always slice it in a slant and I would always wonder why, only to realize this real reason much later!

NINETEEN

Bhee Patata

20 MINS   SERVES 3   MEDIUM

INGREDIENTS

Lotus Roots (washed and cleaned thoroughly; soak in warm water and wash under running water) – 2 to 3 medium sized roots

Potatoes – 2 medium sized

Onions – 2 large (finely chopped)

Tomato – 2 medium sized (finely chopped)

Ginger-Garlic Paste – 2 tbsp

Green Chilis – 2 (finely chopped)

Turmeric Powder – ¼ tsp

Coriander Powder – 1 tsp

Cumin Powder – ½ tsp

Salt – as per taste

Oil – 2 tbsp

Garam Masala – for garnish

Coriander Leaves – for garnish (finely chopped)

Step 1: Clean and slice the Bhee into 1 inch pieces and pressure cook with some salt and water. The number of whistles of the pressure cooker will depend on the quality of the Bhee. Usually these get done in 3 – 4 whistles but sometimes may take longer. Use a fork to check whether it is passing through the piece easily. Drain and keep aside.

Step 2: Peel and chop the potatoes into large sized pieces. Add some salt and keep aside. You could also soak in water to avoid them from turning black.

Step 3: In a heavy bottomed pan, on medium flame, heat the oil and first add the sliced onions and the ginger garlic paste.

Step 4: When onions turn translucent, add the tomatoes and green chilis and sautee for some time. Now add the potato and cook on medium flame.

Step 5: Next, add the turmeric, chili, coriander and cumin powders along with some salt, lower the flame, cover and cook the potatoes until they are almost done.

Step 6: Now add the cooked Bhee pieces, cover and cook. You could also sprinkle some water if spices stick to the pan or the mixture turns too dry. Once the potatoes are done, turn off the flame, garnish with Garam Masala and finely chopped fresh coriander.

While I like Bhee patata dry, you could also add some water and adjust its consistency as you like.

Serve Bhee Patata warm at lunch or dinner with Phulko/Roti.

MOONGAN JI DAL
(Whole green gram Lentil)

Moongan Ji Dal was one of the dals who's taste grew on me. Made exactly like Tidali Dal, the overpowering garlic flavor was one that took its time.

When my mom would make this dal, we would eat it with phulko. Because it was a light dal, the three of us would be slurping away while eating it, enjoying the fun sound and generally competing who would make the louder slurp sound!

Alongside she would usually make patata (as in the sayoon patata recipe). My father would call them "patate jun kachryun" (fried potatoes).

Nowadays we love this dal even just like that. The garlic tempering along with the curry leaves and cumin seeds makes this dal the perfect dal soup. But me, I still eat it with Phulko.

TWENTY

Moongan ji Dal

⏱ 20 MINS   🍽 SERVES 4   👨‍🍳 EASY

INGREDIENTS

Whole Green Gram – 1 cup (soak overnight)

Tomato – 1 medium sized (finely chopped)

Turmeric Powder – ¼ tsp

Ginger – a small piece (grated)

Green Chili – 1 (finely chopped)

Salt – as per taste

FOR TEMPERING

Garlic – 6 to 7 cloves (finely chopped)

Oil – 1 tbsp

Curry Leaves – 4 to 5

Cumin Seeds – 1 tsp

Coriander Leaves – for garnish (finely chopped)

Step 1: In a pressure cooker add the soaked lentils, chopped tomato, chilli, ginger, salt, turmeric and enough water to cover the lentils. Let the lentils cook for at least 5 to 6 whistles or until all the lentils are cooked.

Step 2: Once the cooker depressurizes naturally, open the lid and whisk the lentils.

Step 3: For the tempering, heat the oil in a small frying pan. When hot, add the finely chopped garlic cloves, curry leaves and cumin seeds, in that order. First let the garlic cloves turn golden brown, next immediately add the curry leaves and then the cumin seeds.

Step 4: Once the cumin seeds crackle, add this tempering to the lentils and immediately cover the lentils so that the lentils absorb all the tempering flavors. Let the lentils simmer on low flame with the lid closed for at least 5 minutes.

Step 5: Once you have adjusted the consistency of the lentils, garnish with coriander leaves.

Serve hot at meal time with Dhodho or Phulko or rice.

METHI JI BHAJI
(Fresh Fenugreek Leaves)

My mother would make this dish with Methi, carrots and green peas and very little potatoes making it a very healthy side.

I remember that we would want to just pick the carrots and peas from this bhaji and leave the bitter methi leaves behind! But we would have to finish what was on our plate and so we would just swallow the leaves and run away.

Today I use methi leaves ever so often to make parathas for my son so that the bitterness is camouflaged in the flour but I do make Methi ji Bhaji for my husband and myself many a times especially when I get fresh methi leaves.

I love the fusion of the sweet peas and carrots and the methi leaves. It gives my dish a very earthy feel and of course reminds me of my mother and her efforts to ensure that we always ate healthy food.

Make this dish with Tidali dal and enjoy this healthy and yummy meal!

TWENTY ONE

Methi ji Bhaji

🕐 25 MINS　　　🍴 SERVES 3　　　👨‍🍳 MEDIUM

INGREDIENTS

Fenugreek Leaves (Methi) – 1 cup (washed and chopped finely)

Green Peas – ¼ cup

Carrots – ¼ cup (peeled and chopped in round shape)

Potato – 4 or 5 cubes

Onion – 1 medium sized (finely chopped)

Tomato – 1 medium sized (finely chopped)

Green Chili – 1 (finely chopped)

Garlic – 2 cloves (crushed)

Turmeric Powder – ¼ tsp

Coriander Powder – ½ tsp

Salt – taste

Oil – 1 tbsp

Water – if required

Lemon Juice – 1 tsp

Garam Masala (Optional) – ¼ tsp

Step 1: In a pan, heat the oil, on medium flame and add the onion. When the onion turns translucent, add the methi and let the methi and onions form a nice mixture. Add the garlic and green chili and saute for about 5 minutes.

Step 2: Next add the potatoes, green peas and carrots; cover and cook on low flame for 10 minutes. If required splash some water to prevent the vegetables from sticking to the pan.

Step 3: When these vegetables are almost done, add the tomatoes and spices – turmeric and coriander powder. Cover and cook on low flame until everything comes together and all the vegetables are cooked. Garnish with lemon juice and Garam Masala (if using).

Serve warm at lunch or dinner with Tidali dal or yellow moong dal and enjoy this nutritious meal!

SAI BHAJI
(Green Vegetable)

'Sai' in Sindhi means green and 'Bhaji' means vegetable. Sai Bhaji takes its name from the color of the preparation and no guesses, the queen of this dish is the Spinach. I remember when we went to buy vegetables, this 'trio' would be available with all the vendors – Palak (Spinach) which would be a big bunch along with a small bunch of Methi (Fenugreek leaves) and the smallest Sua (Dil Leaves). Even to this day I look for these three greens and like most Sindhi households, you will find this preparation in my kitchen at least once a week!

This used to be my brother's favorite 'dal' (Lentil preparation) and Mom used to make it almost every Thursday, since it was also 'half-day' of school for him and he would be back from school early. The three of us would relish this hearty lunch after school. Put our bags away, wash our hands and eat in 'steel thalis' with our hands, licking our fingers away; Sai Bhaji, Chanwar (Rice) and Yoghurt. Sometimes there would be papad alongside.

Then we would get ready to do our homework for the day. So here's my mother's recipe of this very loved dish.

TWENTY TWO

Sai Bhaji

🕐 20 MINS   🍴 SERVES 4   👨‍🍳 EASY

INGREDIENTS

Spinach – 1 bunch (washed and chopped)

Split Bengal Gram (Chana Dal) – ½ cup

Onion – 1 medium sized (finely chopped)

Tomatoes – 1 medium sized (finely chopped)

Green Chilis – as per taste

Dil Leaves – ¼ cup

Fenugreek Leaves (the small variety if available; if not use the big ones) – ½ cup

Ginger-Garlic Paste – 1 tbsp

Salt – as per taste

Turmeric Powder – ¼ tsp

Oil – 2 tbsps

I use the pressure cooker to make this easy dish.

Step 1: First heat some oil in the pressure cooker, next add the chopped onions and the ginger-garlic paste.

Step 2: When the onions are translucent, add the tomatoes along with a very small quantity of the fenugreek and dil leaves. Add salt and turmeric powder. Cook this paste until it releases oil.

Step 3: Now add the Spinach and mix well with the onion and tomato paste. Saute for a few minutes; next add the washed split bengal gram and mix well. Saute this for a few minutes too.

Step 4: Next add some warm water. Since spinach releases water add only so much that it just about covers the mixture. Now close the pressure cooker and cook for at least 5 whistles or till the split bengal gram is cooked.

Step 5: Open the cooker only when it naturally depressurizes and mash the split bengal gram and spinach well such that it looks homogenous. Add a few drops of lemon juice just before serving.

Sai Bhaji tastes best with steamed rice or the traditional Bhuga Chanwar (sauteed rice).

BHUGA CHANWAR
(Sauteed Rice)

Bhuga Chanwar makes a perfect combination with Sai Bhaji and Aloo tikki. Alternatively with Charan ji dal. You can find these recipes in this book.

At home, Bhuga Chanwar, Sai Bhaji and Aloo tikki was a traditional lunch when we had guests. The aroma of the caramelized onions, the sizzling of tikkis and the faint scent of dill from the Sai Bhaji - take me back to those wonderful childhood days.

My mother would serve these in a brown ceramic dinner set and I remember we would help her arrange the table; all the time waiting for the guests to leave so that we could pounce on the food especially the Aloo Tikkis!

This traditional Sindhi lunch has become a staple at my home too if I am entertaining guests and want to introduce them to authentic Sindhi food. I am so proud of this combination; it is a complete meal and loved by all my non-Sindhi friends and family too.

TWENTY THREE

Bhuga Chanwar

🕐 25 MINS   🍽 SERVES 3   👨‍🍳 EASY

INGREDIENTS

Rice – 1 cup

Onions – 2 medium sized (finely sliced)

Black Peppercorns – 3 to 4

Bay Leaf – 1

(You can also add 3 to 4 cloves, a small piece of cinnamon stick and 1 or 2 green cardamom. I consider these optional as that is how my mother made it)

Salt – as per taste

Oil – 2 tbsp

Water – 2 cups

Step 1: Wash and soak the rice for at least 30 minutes.

Step 2: In a heavy bottomed pan, heat the oil, add the Bay leaf, sliced onions and peppercorns (if you are using the other spices, add them now). Saute the onions on medium to low heat until they turn brown

Step 3: Next drain all the water from the rice and add the rice to the caramelized onions. Sautee the rice with the onions for at least a few minutes until they also get some of this color.

Ensure that the flame is medium to low all the time.

Step 4: Now add the water (water is always double the quantity of rice) and salt; and increase the flame to high. Once the water comes to a boil, reduce the flame, simmer, cover and cook until the water is absorbed and the rice is cooked.

Serve Bhuga Chanwar with Sai Bhaji or Charan ji Dal. You will love it.

SINDHI KADHI
(Gram Flour Curry with vegetables)

The favorite at parties and get togethers, the Sindhi kadhi is at once delicious and comforting. Memories of my childhood are filled with 'Kadhi Chanwar' (Curry Rice) lunches especially during summer holidays when all of our cousins would come home and spend the vacation days with us.

I remember my cousin would sing a very popular Bollywood song "Mile jo Kadi kadi (which means if each link joins….) but would supplement the phrase with "uske saath chawal bhi" and all of us would join in unison! With this, the line changed to mean "How I wish we got Kadhi (Sindhi Kadhi) and rice along with it".

The aroma of the roasted gram flour filled our home, the warm soupy Kadhi filled our hungry stomachs, and the song filled our hearts with glee! My mom would look at all our energy and smile, happy that we played and bonded and ate and stayed together!

Today when I make this Sindhi comfort food, I also serve it with Sweet Boondi or Aloo Tuk, both of which make a winning combination with the 'Kadhi Chanwar'. Like many Sindhi households, I make this on special occasions, when I have friends and family over or as Sunday lunch.

TWENTY FOUR

Sindhi Kadhi

🕐 40 MINS   🍴 SERVES 4   👨‍🍳 MEDIUM

INGREDIENTS

Gram Flour – ¼ cup

Cooking Oil – 2 to 3 tbsp

Cumin Seeds – ½ tsp

Fenugreek Seeds – ¼ tsp

Mustard Seeds – ½ tsp

Turmeric Powder – ¼ tsp

Curry Leaves – a few

Salt – as per taste

Tamarind Paste – 2 tbsp
or Kokam – 3 to 4 (you could use
the wet or dry variety)

Tomato Pulp – ¼ cup

Water – 3 to 4 hot cups

VEGETABLES

Potato – 1 (peeled and cubed)

Baby carrots – 4 to 5

Cauliflower – a few florets (you can
sautée or fry them in oil beforehand)

Cluster Beans (Gvar) – a few

Okra – a few (fried or sautéed in oil)

Drumsticks – a few, 3" to 4" pieces
(wash and peel the skin)

Step 1: Heat the oil in a heavy bottomed, fairly big sized pan. When the oil is hot, add the cumin, mustard and fenugreek seeds. Lower the flame and add the gram flour. Now roast the gram flour over low flame. The gram flour should be roasted in enough oil so add an additional tablespoon if you need to.

Step 2: Roast the gram flour until it changes color to light golden and releases aroma. Now add 3 to 4 cups of hot water and stir continuously so that there are no lumps. This is a very important step. Add the turmeric and chili powder and the curry leaves and bring the whole mixture to a rolling boil.

Step 3: Next add the Tamarind pulp. If adding Kokams, add them now. I prefer to use Kokam since it gives the Kadhi a very unique tangy flavor. Next add the tomato pulp.

Add the veggies. First add the potatoes; cover and let them cook in the Kadhi for about 15 minutes until they are soft. Add salt.

Step 4: Once the potatoes are almost done, add the rest of the veggies one by one. Cover and cook until all the vegetables are ready.

This very traditional Kadhi is served hot with steamed rice and Aloo Tuk or Sweet Boondi.

GOGRUN JI BHAJI
(Turnips)

Gogru or turnips may not sound appetizing for any kid or even grown up. When we were little my mother would cajole us to eat this vegetable. Try it; you will like it' she would say.

We knew we did not have a choice but we would still turn up our noses and reluctantly sit at the table to eat Gogrun ji Bhaji and Phulko. And we would be pleasantly surprised because it did taste good! With a side of yoghurt and some dal, this would be a perfect after school lunch, healthy and hearty at the same time.

Serve Gogrun ji Bhaji along with yellow Moong Dal or even Charan ji Dal, yoghurt and Sandhyal Basar. It's a simple treat for a hungry tummy.

TWENTY FIVE

Gogrun ji Bhaji

⏱ 20 MINS   🍽 SERVES 4   👨‍🍳 EASY

INGREDIENTS

Turnips – 2 (peeled, chopped and washed)

Onion – 1 medium sized (finely chopped)

Tomatoes – 1 medium sized (finely chopped)

Oil – 2 tbsps

Green Garlic – 5 to 6 cloves with the green stalk (finely chopped)

Green Chili – 1 (finely chopped)

Turmeric Powder – ¼ tsp

Coriander Powder – ½ tsp

Red Chili Powder – ½ tsp

Sugar – ¼ tsp

Water – ½ cup

Salt – as per taste

Coriander Leaves – for garnish

Step 1: In a pressure cooker, heat oil on medium to low flame and first add the onions. When they turn translucent, add the chopped turnips.

Step 2: Once the turnips turn translucent, add all the spices along with the tomatoes and green garlic.

Step 3: Now add the water, close the pressure cooker lid and let the mixture cook for at least 4 whistles.

Step 4: When the cooker depressurizes, open the lid and check if the turnips are completely cooked.

Step 5: If the turnips are completely cooked, using a wooden vegetable masher, mash all of the mixture and on low flame let the mixture dry. Once the mixture releases oil, the Gogrun ji Bhaji is ready.

Garnish with finely chopped coriander leaves.

Serve this bhaji warm at lunch with Phulko and yoghurt

TIDALI DAL
(3 Lentils preparation)

Dals (Lentils) found a place on the table at almost every meal and they still do. Dal, Phulko and Bhaji have been a staple.

Tidali Dal is so called, because it uses three different types of lentils (coming from the word 'te' which means three in Sindhi).

Any three lentils can be used but traditionally we use Bengal Gram Lentils, Black split lentils with skin and Green Split lentils with skin in a specific ratio. Needless to add Tidali dal is very healthy and it also tastes great. Serve it with any Dhodho or rice and you have a perfect meal.

TWENTY SIX

Tidali Dal

⏱ 20 MINS   🍴 SERVES 4   👨‍🍳 EASY

INGREDIENTS

Lentils – 1 cup (Bengal Gram: Black Split Lentils with skin: Green Split Lentils with skin – 1:1:1/4)

Tomato – 1 medium sized (finely chopped)

Turmeric Powder – ¼ tsp

Ginger – a small piece grated

Green Chili – 1 (finely chopped)

Salt – as per taste

FOR TEMPERING

Garlic – 6 to 7 cloves (finely chopped)

Oil – 1 tbsp

Curry Leaves – 4 to 5

Cumin Seeds – 1 tsp

Coriander Leaves – for garnish (finely chopped)

Step 1: Wash and soak the lentils for at least a couple of hours. The in a pressure cooker add these lentils, chopped tomato, chill, ginge salt, turmeric and enough water to cover the lentils. Let the lentil cook for at least 5 to 6 whistles or until all the lentils are cooked.

Step 2: Once the cooker depressurizes naturally, open the lid and whisk the lentils.

Step 3: For the tempering, heat the oil in a small frying pan. Whe hot, add the finely chopped garlic cloves, curry leaves and cumi seeds, in that order. First let the garlic cloves turn golden brown, nex immediately add the curry leaves and then the cumin seeds.

Step 4: Once the cumin seeds crackle, add this tempering to th lentils and immediately cover the lentils so that the lentils absorb a the tempering flavors. Let the lentils simmer on low flame with the li closed for at least 5 minutes.

Step 5: Once you have adjusted the consistency of the lentils, garnis with coriander leaves.

Serve hot at meal time with Dhodho or Phulko or rice.

BHARYAL KARELA
(Stuffed Bitter Gourd)

Karela preparation is one that grows on you. As kids we were not too fond of Karela but as adults now, we savor its taste and especially "Bharyal Karela", which tastes great with Phulko.

We make two types of stuffing for the karela – one which is similar to the one in my recipe Bheendi Patata and the other one which is mentioned here. We also use this stuffing for the Bheendi.

Lets get to the recipe!

TWENTY SEVEN

Bharyal Karela

🕐 45 MINS   🍴 SERVES 3   👨‍🍳 DIFFICUL

INGREDIENTS

Karela (use the small ones) – 3 to 4 (scraped, slit and salted overnight)

Potato – 1 medium sized (sliced lengthwise)

Onions – 1 medium (sliced lengthwise)

Garlic – 8 to 10 cloves

Fresh Coriander – 1 cup

Green Chilis – 2 to 3

Cumin Seeds – ½ tsp

Turmeric Powder – ¼ tsp

Coriander Powder – ½ tsp

Mango Powder – ½ tsp

Salt – as per taste

Oil – 3 to 4 tbsp

Step 1: For the stuffing, using a mortar pestle, coarsely grind cumin seeds, green chilis, garlic cloves and coriander leaves.

Step 2: In this coarsely ground mixture, add salt, turmeric, coriande and mango powders. The stuffing mixture is ready.

Step 3: Wash the salted karela thoroughly. In the slits stuff the mixture and tie the karela with a cotton thread so that the stuffing stays inside when cooking them. Save some stuffing for the potato.

Step 4: In a broad, heavy bottom pan, heat enough oil to shallow fr the karela on medium to low flame taking care that the karela do no turn black. When they are golden brown on all sides, drain them or a kitchen towel.

Step 5: In the same pan, add some more oil if required and lightl sauté the potato slices. When these are a little cooked, add in slice onions and the stuffing mixture. Cover and cook the potatoes, stirring intermittently.

Step 6: When potatoes are almost done, add the shallow fried stuffed karela. Cover and cook until both the vegetables are completel cooked.

Serve warm at meal time with Phulko and a side of yoghurt.

PHOOLPATASHA
(Dried Lotus Seeds)

Phoolpatasha curry remains a hot favorite among all us Sindhis. Tastes great and is so easy to make! You can serve it with Bhuga Chanwar or Phulko, and with a side of yoghurt, you have a complete and wholesome meal.

As kids, during the monsoons, my grandfather would bring the green fresh pods of lotus and we would all love to munch upon the fresh lotus seeds. It has been years that we have eaten those and how I long to taste the fresh green seeds again.

The dried lotus seeds are called Phoolpatasha and used in curries. My mother made Phoolpatasha curry occasionally; it was more like festive food and we would eat it with Phulko. The Phoolpatasha were so soft once cooked, they would melt in our mouths, and we would be slurping the gravy!

Garnished with coriander, this dish is beautiful to look at and divine to serve!

TWENTY EIGHT

Phoolpatasha

20 MINS   SERVES 3   MEDIUM

INGREDIENTS

Phoolpatasha/Dried Lotus Seeds – 1 cup

Onions – 2 medium sized

Tomatoes – 2 medium sized

Ginger-Garlic Paste – 2 tbsp

Turmeric Powder – ¼ tsp

Coriander Powder – ½ tsp

Green Chilis – 1 (finely chopped)

Salt – as per taste

Oil – 1 tbsp

Water – as required

Coriander Leaves – for garnish (finely chopped)

Step 1: First, grind the onions and tomatoes separately. Next, in a pressure cooker, heat some oil, add the onion paste, ginger-garlic paste, and finely chopped green chili.

Step 2: Sprinkle some water in case the onion paste sticks to the bottom of the cooker. When the onion paste turns brown, add the tomatoes. Next, add the salt, turmeric and coriander powders and sauté until the mixture releases oil.

Step 3: Add the Phoolpatasha and mix them into this onion tomato mixture. Now add water only enough to barely cover the Phoolpatasha and cook for about 3 whistles.

Once the pressure cooker naturally depressurizes, open it, adjust the consistency of the gravy and garnish with some finely chopped fresh coriander.

Serve warm at lunch with Phulko or Roti. Or you could also serve it with Bhuga Chanwar.

BESAN JI BHAJI
(Gram Flour Veggie)

Besan ji Bhaji literally means Gram Flour Vegetable, but this dish is made of deep fried gram flour tikkis (patties). Also called Aani ji Bhaji/Besan Tikki ji Bhaji/Aani Basar, this is a mouth-watering main course.

My mother often made this dish when we had guests and other times when there was no other vegetable in the house except the usual onions and tomatoes. She also knew of our love for the fried tikkis (patties) (before they were dunked into the curry) so she would always save us, one each, so we could eat those with ketchup!

Of course, we loved the onion dominated curry with a faint flavor of all the spices and along with phulko we would be a very delighted and satiated three kids!

Besan ji Bhaji is loved by my family and even my non-Sindhi friends motivating me to make it frequently even though it is a lengthy preparation.

TWENTY NINE

Besan ji Bhaji

⏱ 60 MINS · 🍽 SERVES 3 · 👨‍🍳 DIFFICUL

INGREDIENTS

FOR THE TIKKIS (PATTIES)

Gram Flour (Besan) – 1 cup

Poppy Seeds – 1 tbsp

Green Chilis – 2 (finely chopped)

Onion – 1 small sized (finely chopped)

Coriander Leaves – few (finely chopped)

Red Chili Powder – ½ tsp

Coriander Powder – 1 tsp

Salt – as per taste

Oil – 2 to 3 tbsp or as required as explained in the recipe

Oil – to deep-fry the tikkis (Patties)

Water

Step 1: To make the tikkis (patties), in a mixing bowl, combine the gram flour (besan), finely chopped onion, poppy seeds, finely chopped green chilis, coriander leaves, red chili and coriander powders and salt.

(I add finely chopped onions to the tikkis but this is optional)

Step 2: To make a stiff dough of this mixture, first add enough oil – 2 tbsps or more so the mixture resembles breadcrumbs. The way to check if you have added enough oil is that when you hold the mixture in your palm and press it with your fingers, the mixture holds shape. Add absolutely minimal water to make the dough. Divide the dough into equal portions and shape each portion into an oval shaped tikki

Step 3: Heat some oil. When it is hot, add the tikkis and lower the flame to medium so that the tikkis are cooked on the inside too. When these are golden brown on both sides, drain them on a kitchen towel and keep aside.

Note – first always fry one tikki to check. If it does not break, then fry the rest of them. If it breaks then it means that the oil in the dough is too much; so just add some more gram flour and knead the dough again before shaping it into tikkis.

INGREDIENTS

FOR THE CURRY

Onions – 3 medium sized (finely chopped)

Tomatoes – 2 (finely chopped)

Ginger-Garlic Paste – 1 tbsp

Green Chilis – 1 or 2 (finely chopped)

Turmeric Powder – ¼ tsp

Coriander Powder – ½ tsp

Red Chili Powder – ¼ tsp

Mango Powder – ¼ tsp

Salt – as per taste

Coriander Leaves – some (finely chopped for garnish)

Oil – 2 tbsp

Water

Step 4: To make the curry for these tikkis, in a heavy bottom pan, first heat some oil. When hot, on medium flame, add finely chopped onions and fry until they are pink and translucent. Next, add the ginger-garlic paste and the finely chopped green chilis.

Step 5: Add the finely chopped tomatoes and all the spices – turmeric, red chili, mango and coriander powders- and salt. Keep stirring and let this mixture cook on medium flame until it releases oil.

Step 6: At this time, on low flame, add the fried tikkis and mix them well into the mixture. Do not stir too hard otherwise the tikkis may break. Let the tikkis cook in this mixture for about 5 to 10 minutes on low flame so that they can absorb all the spices and flavors.

Step 6: Next add hot water enough to barely cover the tikkis, cover and cook on medium to low flame, stirring every 5 minutes and also gently flipping the tikkis.

Step 7: After about 10 – 15 minutes, check if the tikkis are cooked. Once they are, switch off the flame and garnish with coriander leaves and optionally some garam masala. This dish is neither too wet nor too dry so ensure this consistency.

Serve besan ji bhaji warm with Phulko.

SINDHI RAJMA
(Sindhi style Kidney Beans)

Rajma is a very popular type of bean used in Indian cooking. My mother made this as a lunch meal and we loved to eat this with Phulko and a side of yoghurt.

The special note about this recipe is that she never made Rajma by itself. She always mixed 'maahe ji dal' (Whole Black lentils), so the creamy texture came from 'maahe ji dal' whilst Rajma was still the main aspect of the dish.

Today I also add fresh cream for a richer taste especially when we are entertaining and have guests over, but my mother made it with the basic ingredients, probably the reason why it tasted so earthy, so hearty and so flavorful.

Try this very special recipe from my mother's kitchen and I am sure you will love it.

THIRTY

Sindhi Rajma

75 MINS   SERVES 3   DIFFICULT

INGREDIENTS

Rajma (Kidney Beans) – ¼ cup

Maahe ji Dal (Whole Black Lentils/ Whole Urad Dal) – ¼ cup

Onions – 1 medium sized (blend it and make a paste)

Tomatoes – 2 medium sized (make a puree)

Ginger-Garlic Paste – 1 tbsp

Hing (Asoefetida) – a pinch

Cumin Seeds – ½ tsp

Turmeric Powder – ¼ tsp

Coriander Powder – ½ tsp

Water – to cook the lentils and beans and adjust consistency

OPTIONAL:

Kasuri Methi (Dried Fenugreek Leaves) – ¼ tp

Garam Masala – ¼ tsp

Fresh Cream – 1 to 2 tbsp

Ghee – 1.5 tbsp

Step 1: Soak the lentils and kidney beans overnight. Drain the water and add the soaked lentils and beans in a pressure cooker. Cover them with water at least an inch or two above their surface. Add turmeric powder and salt and pressure-cook them on high flame for at least 7 to 8 whistles or until they are completely cooked.

Step 3: Switch off the flame and open the lid only when the cooker has completely depressurized naturally. Check whether the lentils and the beans are cooked. You can also mash a few of the grains.

Step 4: In a heavy bottomed pan, on medium flame, heat the ghee add the cumin seeds and hing. When the cumin seeds crackle, add the onion paste and sautee it until it turns light brown. Add the ginger garlic paste.

Step 5: When the raw smell of the ginger and garlic is gone, add the tomato puree and spices – coriander and red chili powders.

Keep stirring the onion-tomato and spice mixture on medium flame, until it releases oil and leaves the sides of the pan. Now add the boiled lentils and beans and mix well.

Step 6: Add some hot water in order to adjust the consistency of the preparation and keep stirring the Rajma and Dal on medium heat for at least 30 minutes. The more this dal simmers, the better its texture becomes.

Step 7: If adding Kasuri Methi and Garam Masala, add it now after the preparation has simmered for at least 30 minutes.

Step 8: After adding Kasuri Methi and Garam Masala, let the Rajma and Dal simmer for another 20 to 25 minutes before adding the fresh cream.

Sindhi style Rajma is served at lunch with Phulko or Chanwar.

BHARYAL SHIMLA MIRCH
(Stuffed Bell Pepper/Capsicum)

The aroma of roasted bell pepper takes me back to my childhood days when we would wait for this dish. Roasted bell pepper stuffed with flavored potato, eaten with Phulko never tasted so good! So delightfully flavorful we kids would love this dish.

My mother would make it in her iron 'tayi' (frying pan) and we would be so impatient that we would want to eat it straight from the pan without even waiting for her to plate it!

Served mostly alongside Charan ji Dal, this delightful combination makes me drool even today! So here's the recipe for this dish. Now, I am not sure if this is a strictly Sindhi preparation, but this is my mother's recipe and you will love it.

THIRTY ONE

Bharyal Shimla Mirch

30 MINS   SERVES 2   MEDIUM

INGREDIENTS

Capsicum/Bell Pepper – 2

Potatoes – 3-4 medium sized boiled and peeled

Mustard Seeds – ¼ tsp

Turmeric Powder – ¼ tsp

Green Chili – 1 (finely chopped)

Coriander Powder – ½ tsp

Mango Powder – ¼ tsp

Salt – as per taste

Coriander Leaves – finely chopped

Oil – 2 to 3 tbsp

Step 1: First, clean the capsicum. Slice the top and scrape the seeds to get the hollow space for the stuffing.

Step 2: For the stuffing, mash the boiled potatoes. Heat oil in a pan and add the mustard seeds. When they crackle, lower the flame and add the turmeric powder, curry leaves and the mashed potatoes. Mix well.

Step 3: Add salt, coriander and mango powders. Then add the finely chopped fresh coriander leaves. Cover and cook on low flame and let the stuffing come together. Let the potatoes turn brown at the bottom of the pan (taro lagarn in Sindhi). Then switch off the flame.

Step 4: Stuff the bell peppers with this mixture and now shallow fry the peppers with little oil on low flame. Keep tossing the bell peppers at regular intervals so that they are well roasted from all sides.

Step 5: Once the bell peppers are well roasted, switch off the flame.

Serve warm at meal time with Phulko and any dal. My preferred one is Charan ji Dal!

KADU-A-JA KOFTA
(Bottle Gourd Balls in Curry)

Koftas are abundant in Indian cuisine and Kadu-a-ja koftas find a special place in the Sindhi cuisine. Kofta is such a nice way to camouflage a vegetable and turn it into something fun and yummy.

I never liked Kadu as a kid but I remember I would wait for my mother to make these koftas not knowing that it is the same vegetable! And I would love to eat them especially before they were dunked into the curry. Before she knew it, I would run away with a couple of the deep-fried koftas in my hands and pop them in my mouth! I always thought they were pakoras!

Now I even, have the opportunity to turn these into a healthier option by making the koftas in my appe/paniyaram pan instead of deep-frying them! You could do either and they both taste great. Of course deep-frying them is the traditional method but you could also shallow fry them or like me, use the appe pan.

Serve Kadu-a-ja kofta with Phulko. It is a complete meal!

THIRTY TWO

Kadu-a-ja Kofta

45 MINS   SERVES 3   DIFFICULT

INGREDIENTS

FOR 6 KOFTAS

Bottle Gourd (Kadu) – ½ large sized

Gram Flour – 2 to 4 tbsps

Coriander Leaves – ¼ cup

Green Chili – 1 (finely chopped)

Salt – as per taste

Red Chili Powder – ½ tsp

Black Pepper Powder – ¼ tsp

Cumin Powder – ½ tsp

Coriander Powder – ½ tsp

Mango Powder – ¼ tsp

Lemon Juice – ¼ tsp

Ghee – ½ tbsp

FOR THE CURRY

Onion – 1 medium sized

Tomato – 1 medium sized

Ginger – 1 inch

Garlic – 3 to 4 cloves

Green Chili – 1

Green Cardamom – 2

Black Cardamom – 1

Cloves – 2

Black Peppercorns – 2

Cinnamon Stick – ½ inch

Turmeric Powder – ¼ tsp

Cumin Powder – ½ tsp

Coriander Powder – ½ tsp

Red Chili Powder – ¼ tsp

Gram Flour – 2 tbsps

FOR GARNISH

Dried Fenugreek Leaves (Kasuri Methi) – ¼ tsp

Garam Masala (optional) – ¼ tsp

Coriander Leaves – finely chopped

Step 1: Grate the bottle gourd. Using a muslin cloth, drain excess water from the bottle gourd. Retain this water to use in the curry.

Step 2: To the grated bottled gourd, add finely chopped coriander leaves, green chili, some lemon juice and the spices – chili, coriander, cumin, black pepper and mango powders. Add salt to taste.

Step 3: Add ghee and gram flour, mix well and make small balls/kofta. If the mixture does not bind, add more gram flour.

Step 4: Grease each mould in the ape/panyaram pan, and add one ball/kofta in each mould. Roast the koftas in the pan on low flame turning the koftas at regular intervals so that they are evenly roasted. You could also deep-fry them.

Step 5: Meanwhile prepare the curry. In a heavy bottom pan, heat some oil on medium flame and add finely chopped onions. In a mortal pestle coarsely pound the cinnamon stick, pepper corns, black and green cardamoms and cloves and add them to the chopped onions.

Step 6: Grind tomatoes, ginger, garlic and green chili and add them to the onions after the onions have turned brown. Sauté the onion tomato mixture until it releases oil.

Step 7: Lower the flame, add the gram flour and roast it in the onion tomato mixture until it loses its raw smell. Add the spices – turmeric, red chili, coriander, cumin and add the bottle gourd water drained out in step 1. Now sauté this mixture until it releases oil and the water dries up completely. This means the spices and gram flour have all cooked well.

Step 8: Add some water and let the mixture come to a boil. The curry is ready. Add the koftas. Garnish with Kasuri Methi, Garam Masala (if using) and coriander leaves. Cover and cook for about 15 minutes on low flame.

Serve immediately. Since the koftas are not fried, do not leave them in the curry for too long before serving.

Serve Kofta warm at lunch time with Phulko.

TURI JI BHAJI
(Ridge Gourd Preparation)

Turi or Ridge Gourd is a very common vegetable in any Sindhi household. One because it is very easy to make and two because it tastes very good.

Looks can definitely be deceptive and while Turi does not look appetizing, it tastes great; and there are so many ways to make it. Turi by itself tastes very nice but because it reduces so much when cooking that a very common style is to mix it with any of the Dals (Lentils), usually Bengal Gram and make it a dry dish.

Either way, it tastes great and has so many benefits that I find myself making Turi (Ridge Gourd) quite often.

As kids though I will admit, my mother had to request, force and cajole!!! But, we did not have a choice and we simply had to follow her instructions and I am always glad we did.

Here is the recipe that I learnt from my mother. I serve it with Phulka a side of Dal and yoghurt.

THIRTY THREE

Turi ji Bhaji

🕐 25 MINS   🍴 SERVES 2   👨‍🍳 EASY

INGREDIENTS

Ridge Gourd – 2 medium sized (Note that Ridge Gourd reduces when cooked so use accordingly)

Onions – 1 medium sized (finely chopped)

Tomatoes – 1 medium sized (finely chopped)

Green Chili – 1 (finely chopped)

Garlic – 4 to 5 cloves (crushed)

Ginger – ½ tsp grated

Turmeric Powder – ¼ tsp

Coriander Powder – ½ tsp

Mango Powder – ¼ tsp

Salt – as per taste

Oil – 1 ½ tbsp.

Water – 1 ½ tbsp

Coriander Leaves – for garnish (finely chopped)

Step 1: Peel the ridge gourd and cut the gourd into small cubes.

Step 2: In a pressure cooker, heat some oil on low flame. Add the finely chopped onions and sauté until they turn light golden brown before adding the ginger and garlic.

Step 2: Add the tomatoes, green chili and the spices - turmeric, coriander, mango powders and salt. Sauté this onion tomato mixture until the tomatoes turn mushy and the mixture releases oil.

Step 3: Now add the chopped ridge gourd pieces and cook them on low flame in this mixture for a few minutes. Then add the 1½ tbsps of water. Ridge gourd itself has a lot of water so you don't need to add anymore.

Step 4: Now close the pressure cooker lid and on high flame cook the ridge gourd for at least 4 to 5 whistles and then switch off the flame.

Step 5: Open the lid of the pressure cooker when it depressurizes naturally. Check if the ridge gourd is cooked completely and if it has, on low flame, dry off any excess water. Garnish with finely chopped fresh coriander leaves.

Serve hot with Phulka, any dal (lentils), and a side of yoghurt.

MACROLI PATATA
(Macroni and Potatoes)

Macroli Patata is yet another signature dish of the Sindhis. I don't know how this combination became such as integral part of the Sindhi Cuisine but there it is...macaroni made with Potatoes in a curry!

I remember my mother making it quite often. We would get 'elbow Macaroni' from a regular 'kirana' (a small neighborhood retail store), store and my mother would make this dish quite often. Served with Phulko, this dish tasted delicious and I remember my old grandmother relishing it too!

When I make it now, my son who loves his pastas, looks at me in wonderment! And me, I am a happy mother to see him finish, that which is served on his plate.

THIRTY FOUR

Macroli Patata

🕐 20 MINS   🍴 SERVES 3   👨‍🍳 EASY

INGREDIENTS

Macaroni – ½ cup

Potatoes – 1 medium sized diced

Green Peas – a handful

Onions – 1 medium sized (finely chopped)

Tomatoes – 2 medium sized (puree)

Ginger – 1 tsp

Garlic – 3 to 4 cloves (crushed)

Turmeric Powder – ¼ tsp

Coriander Powder – ½ tsp

Red Chili Powder – ¼ tsp

Oil – 2 tbsp

Water – 2 cups

Coriander Leaves – for garnish (finely chopped)

Garam Masala – ¼ tsp for garnish

Step 1: In a pressure cooker on medium flame, heat the oil. Add the onions, ginger and garlic and sauté till the onions turn light golden brown.

Step 2: Next add the tomato puree and the spices – turmeric coriander and red chili powders. Add salt.

Step 3: Keep stirring this mixture until the rawness of the spices is replaced by their aroma and the mixture starts releasing oil.

Step 4: Add the diced potatoes, macaroni and peas and stir them into the mixture. Add water and close the pressure cooker. On high flame cook the potatoes, macaroni and peas for 3 to 4 whistles or until they are cooked.

Step 5: Switch off the flame and open the lid of the cooker only when it depressurizes naturally. Then garnish with garam masala and finely chopped fresh coriander leaves.

Serve warm at lunch with Phulko.

SINDHI KHICHREEN
(Savory porridge made with Rice and Lentils)

Khichreen is a one-pot meal, healthy and tasty at the same time. Typically, khichdi preparations use many vegetables cooked along with rice and lentils.

Served usually with yoghurt, the watery and light Sindhi khichreen is made from rice and split green moong lentils only. Sides could include fried vegetables, papad, or pickle.

As kids we would love eating this really hot khichdi (straight after the pressure cooker had depressurized) on our thali (plate) with a dollop of really cold yoghurt sprinkled with some black pepper, the now warm Khichreen comforting our souls!

Especially during our summer holidays, this would be a quick meal before we could go back to playing with our friends!

Today I do the same for my son! This is a quick, healthy and hearty meal before my son can go back to playing with his friends…

THIRTY FIVE

Sindhi Khichreen

⏱ 30 MINS   🍽 SERVES 2   👨‍🍳 EASY

INGREDIENTS

Rice – ¼ cup

Lentils – ½ cup (you can change the dal to rice ratio)

Ghee – 1 tbsp

Whole Peppercorns – 5 to 6 (coarsely crushed)

Salt – as per taste

Water – 2 cups

Green Cardamoms (Optional) – 2 to 3 (lightly crushed)

Step 1: Wash and soak the rice and lentils together for at least 20 minutes. In a pan, on medium flame, heat the ghee. When it is hot, add the crushed peppercorns. If using cardamom, add it too (I usually don't use cardamom).

Step 2: Drain the soaked rice and lentils and add them to the ghee, sauté them for about a minute or two.

Step 3: Add water and salt and cook on medium flame. Once the water comes to a boil, lower the flame, cover and cook.

Step 4: Check after 15 to 20 minutes. Khichreen should be ready. Add water to adjust consistency if required and cook for another few minutes.

Step 5: Switch off the flame and serve hot.

I serve this with yoghurt, Bhee-a-ja Pakora (Lotus Root Fritters) and Taryal Wangarn (Fried Eggplant). Enjoy!

MAKHNI DAL
(Buttery Lentils)

Makhni in this Sindhi preparation stands for the buttery, creamy texture of the lentils and not the actual use of butter.

Makhni Dal was made often at home, and mostly as Sunday breakfast with Puris (deep fried bread). The aroma of the spices sizzling from the tempering would fill our home on a lazy Sunday morning and we would rush to the kitchen and await the hot fluffed up puris! Mom would always serve us first and pamper us with fresh hot puris, refilling our little katoris (bowls) with dal.

Dal and Puri is the proverbial comfort food - hearty, tasty, simple and filled with nostalgia. Sprinkled all over with colourful spices and garnished with some coriander leaves, this appetizing dal leaves you asking for more.

I serve this dal with puris and sometimes with Toast (Dal Toast - a delicious Sindhi street food).

THIRTY SIX

Makhni Dal

⏱ 20 MINS   🍽 SERVES 2   👨‍🍳 EASY

INGREDIENTS

Moong Dal (petite yellow lentils) – ½ cup

Water – 1 cup

Turmeric Powder – ¼ tsp

Mango Powder – ¼ tsp

Coriander Powder – ½ tsp

Black Pepper Powder – ¼ tsp

Red Chili Powder – ¼ tsp

Cumin Powder – ¼ tsp

Oil – 1 tbsp

Cumin Seeds – ½ tsp

Salt – as per taste

Coriander Leaves - for garnish (finely chopped)

Step 1: Wash and soak the lentils for about 30 minutes. After they are soaked, in a pan, on medium flame, boil the lentils in water and add salt and turmeric powder.

Step 2: While the lentils are cooking, skim off the foam that rises to the top. When the lentils are cooked, whisk them up and switch off the flame.

Step 3: Pour the dal in a serving bowl and now sprinkle all the spices with your fingers all over the lentils – coriander powder, red chili powder, mango powder, powdered black pepper, cumin powder.

Step 4: In a smaller pan, heat some oil and put the cumin seeds. When they crackle, pour this hot oil all over the sprinkled spices on the dal. Garnish with finely chopped fresh coriander leaves.

Serve this dal warm at breakfast or lunch with hot puris.

WANGARN PATATA
(Egg Plant and Potatoes)

Wangarn Patata is a loved side dish in a Sindhi household eaten alongside Dal and Phulko or Dal and Chanwar.

Very easy to prepare with basic ingredients, here's a recipe that you can make anytime.

THIRTY SEVEN

Wangarn Patata

20 MINS   SERVES 3   EASY

INGREDIENTS

Onions – 1 large (finely chopped)

Tomato – 1 medium size (finely chopped)

Green Chili – 1 (finely chopped)

Potato – 1 medium sized (peeled and cut into wedges)

Egg Plant – 2 small sized (cut lengthwise into wedges)

Turmeric Powder – ¼ tsp

Coriander Powder – ½ tsp

Red Chili Powder – ½ tsp

Coriander Leaves – for garnish (finely chopped)

Oil – 1 tbsp

Water – as required

Step 1: In a pan, heat some oil, on medium flame and add the chopped onions. When the onions turn translucent, add the potatoe and salt. Cover and cook for about 5 to 10 minutes on low flame Keep stirring so that the onions do not stick at the bottom of the pan

Step 2: Open the pan; add the eggplant and tomatoes. Add the spices – turmeric, coriander and red chili powders. Add just 2 to 3 tbsps of water if required.

Step 3: Cover and cook until the eggplant is done. Garnish with finely chopped fresh coriander leaves.

Serve this dish at lunch, warm with with Phulko and a side o yoghurt.

SINDHI WADIYUN/ WADI
(Sundried dumplings)

Wadi or Wadiyun are sun-dried dumplings that are used in different curries like Potato Curry or Bhee Curry. They add crunch, flavor and texture to a curry.

Usually these are available at stores but I like to make them myself; It does not take too much time and they are easy to too. It does take time to dry them though since they have to be dried in the sun and this may take 6 to 7 days!

But, in the end, patience pays and these Wadiyun turn out really nice- earthy, crunchy and of course homemade!

THIRTY EIGHT

Sindhi Wadiyun

🕐 30 MINS 🍴 12 PIECES 👨‍🍳 MEDIUM

INGREDIENTS

Split and Skinless Black Lentils (Urad Dal) – 1 cup

Bay Leaf – 1

Fennel Seeds – ½ tsp

Cumin Seeds – ½ tsp

Coriander Seeds – ½ tsp

Asafoetida (Hing) – a pinch

Red Chili Powder – ½ tsp

Black Cardamom Seeds – 1

Black Pepper – ½ tsp

Salt – as per taste

Water

Step 1: Soak the Dal (lentils) in water overnight or at least 3 to 4 hours. Using very little water (2 to 3 tbsps) blend the lentils into a paste.

Step 2: Once the lentils are blended to a paste, add all the spices mentioned above. Now whisk the lentils continuously for at least 10 to 15 minutes until the paste turns into a light and fluffy batter.

Step 3: Wet you fingers with water, take small portions of this light and fluffy batter, and place the dumplings on a plastic/parchment sheet.

Step 4: Make these dumplings with all of the batter and place the plastic/parchment sheet in the sun to dry them. These take at least 6 to 7 days to be completely dry. You can then use them in different curries.

WADIYUN PATATA/ WADI PATATA
(Lentil Dumplings and Potatoes)

I find this dish in so many videos currently doing the rounds where each person points at the Sindhi dish that she has made and Wadi Patata shares the space with other Sindhi delicacies like Sai Bhaji, Dal Pakwan, Tahiri and many others.

I do not remember eating this dish earlier but the more I saw these videos, the more curious it made me and while making Wadi is not new to me given that 'Bodi' is commonly used in the Bengali cuisine too, this Sindhi dish took me sometime to perfect.

With some help from the "Sindhi Rasoi" channel on You Tube, I was able to get and make a perfect Wadi Patata dish. Enjoy this dish with Phulko or even rice. The unique way in which the gravy/curry is made make this dish a sure winner!

THIRTY NINE

Wadiyun Patata

⏱ 30 MINS   🍴 SERVES 4   👨‍🍳 MEDIUM

INGREDIENTS

Wadiyun/Wadi - (4 to 6)

Potato – 1 medium sized (peeled and cut lengthwise into 4 pieces)

Onion – 1 medium sized (finely chopped)

Tomato – 1 medium sized (finely chopped)

Garlic – 2 to 3 cloves (crushed)

Bay Leaves – 2

Turmeric Powder – ¼ tsp

Coriander Powder – ½ tsp

Red Chili Powder – ¼ tsp

Garam Masala Powder – ½ tsp

Coriander Leaves – for garnish

Hing – a pinch

Salt – as per taste

Mustard Oil – 2 tbsps
(Use vegetable oil if mustard oil is not available)

Step 1: In a pressure cooker on medium flame, heat the mustard oil, add hing and next the chopped onions. Onions should turn into a nice brown color before adding the tomato and the garlic cloves.

Step 2: When the tomatoes turn mushy, add the spices – turmeric, coriander and red chili powders – and salt. Mix well and continue to sauté until the onion-tomato mixture comes together and releases oil. Now add some water, close the pressure cooker and on high flame cook this mixture for about 2 to 3 whistles.

Step 3: When the pressure cooker depressurizes naturally, open the lid and using a dal or potato masher, mash this mixture well so that everything comes together and looks like one thick sauce.

Step 4: Now add the potato slices and bay leaves. Sauté the potatoes well in the onion-tomato sauce on medium to low flame. Just before adding the Wadis (lentil dumplings), soak in water for a few minutes.

Step 5: Add the wadis and sauté them, then cover and cook. Do this on medium to low flame and keep checking and stirring.

Do this a few times such that the sauce sticks to the bottom of the pressure cooker. It should not burn, but just toast (taro lagarn as called in Sindhi). Keep scraping this mixture from the bottom of the cooker and continue to cover and cook. This method will give the sauce a very nice toasted smell and a lovely brown color.

Step 6: When the wadis and potatoes have been sautéed sufficiently in this sauce, add some water, close the lid of the pressure cooker and cook on high flame for about 2 to 3 whistles. Once the cooker depressurizes naturally open and check whether the wadis are cooked and soft. If they are, then remove the wadi patata in a serving bowl. Garnish with Garam Masala and fresh coriander leaves and serve.

Serve warm with Phulko.

PEAS AIN PANEER
(Green Peas and Cottage Cheese)

Who does not like Peas ain Paneer? One of our favorite dishes and enjoyed by everyone. This was a very special dish and my mother made this especially when we were expecting guests in her own unique way, since we did not have a blender or mixer for quite a long time. Much later, she used the mixer to blend onions and other spices. For a long time she did that on a big stone.

But, coming back to the recipe, we got the Paneer from a famous dairy shop nearby and she would always lightly fry the Paneer pieces and the gravy was always smooth. She used the grater to grate both the onions and tomatoes and the other spices on the stone.

So it was only fair that she made this dish when we had guests coming over. All of us loved this special preparation and we would wait for her to make this dish…But I think I had a penchant of taking 1 or 2 fried paneer pieces when she wasn't looking and pop them into my mouth. I just loved them like that and I still do!

Nowadays I do not fry paneer pieces but to recreate this recipe I occasionally do and thank my mother for leaving these lovely memories with me!

FORTY

Peas ain Paneer

⏱ 30 MINS   🍽 SERVES 3   👨‍🍳 MEDIUM

INGREDIENTS

Green Peas – 1 ½ cup

Paneer – 150gms

Onion – 1 medium sized (grated)

Tomatoes – 1 medium sized (grated)

Garlic – 3 to 4 cloves

Ginger – 1 inch

Green Chili - 1

Turmeric Powder – ¼ tsp

Coriander Powder – ½ tsp

Homemade Garam Masala (recipe in this book) – 1 tsp

Coriander Leaves – ¼ cup finely chopped

Salt – as per taste

Oil – 1 ½ tbsp

Water as required

Step 1: Fry paneer pieces and keep aside. In a mortal pestle, crush the ginger, chili and garlic into a paste.

Step 2: In a pan, heat oil on medium flame and first add the grated onions. Sauté the onions until they turn translucent and add the ginger, garlic and chili paste. Sauté until there's no raw smell from the garlic or ginger.

Step 3: Next add the grated tomatoes and the spices – turmeric and coriander powders, salt and the homemade garam masala. Also, add some of the finely chopped fresh coriander leaves. Keep stirring until the mixture releases oil and leaves the sides of the pan.

Step 4: Add the green peas and sauté in this mixture for at least 5 minutes. Then add some water and let the green peas cook in this mixture. When the green peas are cooked completely, add the fried paneer pieces. Cover and cook for at least 5 to 7 minutes.

Step 5: Switch off the flame and garnish with fresh coriander leaves.

Serve with Phulko or Puri and enjoy this very traditional peas ain paneer dish sans fresh cream or butter or Ghee or Kasuri Methi.

SINDHI CHOLA
(Sindhi Chick Peas Curry)

Chola is such a versatile preparation. I can pair it with so many snacks or main dishes and whip up a full meal or brunch! Chola with Tikki, Samosa, Kachori, Puri and even Aloo or any other stuffed Paratha tastes great and enhances the dish manifold.

But our favorite combination is Chola with bread! The way we have it at our birthdays with family and friends; love, blessings and wishes in abundance. Try it; bread, topped with Chola, garnished with some finely chopped onions, a dash of the green spicy and date & tamarind chutneys and some nylon 'sev'. And just dig into the yumminess!

As kids we would gobble Chola and bread; there was no garnish, no chutneys, but the taste would always be perfect. Made simple and with love, just like how mothers make it.

FORTY ONE

Sindhi Chola

🕐 45 MINS   🍴 SERVES 4   👨‍🍳 MEDIUM

INGREDIENTS

Chola (Chick Peas) – 1 cup (soaked overnight)

Onions – 2 medium sized

Tomatoes – 2 medium sized

Green Chilis – 2 (finely chopped)

Ginger-Garlic Paste – 1 tbsp

Tamarind paste – 1.5 tbsps

Coriander Leaves – ¼ cup (finely chopped)

Turmeric Powder – ¼ tsp

Coriander Powder – ½ tsp

Red Chili Powder – ½ tsp

Mango Powder – ½ tsp

Chole Masala – 1 tsp

Garam Masala – ½ tsp

Salt – as per taste

Water

Oil – 2 tbsp

Step 1: Boil the soaked Chola in a pressure cooker with water and salt. If you want the Chola to have a dark color, add some Tea water too. Traditionally we never added Tea water but occasionally I add this to render a dark brown color to the Chola. Cook the Chola for about 5 to 6 whistles until they are soft. (Note that the number of whistles may differ based on the quality of the Chola.)

Step 2: Grind the onions and tomatoes separately. In a heavy bottom pan, on medium flame, heat the oil, add the onion and ginger garlic pastes, and roast until the onion paste turns light brown. Sprinkle water if the paste sticks to the bottom of the pan.

Step 3: Next add the tomato paste and chilis and mix well. Now add all the spices (salt, turmeric, coriander, chili, mango powders, Chole Masala and Garam Masalas) and saute this onion-tomato mixture until it releases the oil.

Step 4: Now add in the boiled Chola and mix well with the onion tomato and spice mix. Add the tamarind paste now. Lower the flame and keep stirring the Chola in this mixture for about 10 minutes.

Step 5: Now increase to a medium flame and add water to adjust the consistency of the Chola. You can also mash some of the Chola for a desired consistency. Let the Chola come to a boil; sprinkle some Garam Masala, switch off the flame, cover, and let the Chola rest for some time.

Step 6: Garnish with finely chopped fresh coriander before serving.

Serve Chola warm with Tikki or Dabal (Bread) or Parathas or Puris

CHEHRI PURI AIN PAPAD
(Savory fried bread with Papad)

Puris are a universally loved food. At all parties, all occasions puris are served along with a variety of dishes - Chola (spicy chickpeas), aloo dum (potatoes), dal (lentils) and many others.

However, Chehri Puri can be eaten just like that because it tastes that good. My mother always served it with fried papad! I know that is a lot of deep fried food, but she made this only occasionally and boy how we waited for those occasions!

Chehri Puri ain Papad is my favorite comfort food and it will be yours too once you have tried it!

FORTY TWO

Chehri Puri ain Papad

🕐 25 MINS 🍴 SERVES 4 👨‍🍳 MEDIUM

INGREDIENTS

Wheat Flour – 1 cup

Oil – ½ tbsp for kneading dough and more for deep frying

Salt – ¼ tsp

Black Pepper Powder – ¼ tsp

Cumin Seeds – ½ tsp

Step 1: In a large mixing bowl, mix and combine all the ingredients well. Knead a tight dough using water.

Step 2: With a rolling pin, roll the dough into circles of about the size of your palm and they should be a little thicker than Rotis or Tortillas.

Step 3: Heat oil in a deep frying pan. To check if the oil is ready, drop a pinch of the dough. If it fries and comes up immediately, the oil is ready.

Step 4: Now fry all the Puris. They should fluff up nicely and turn golden brown on both sides; drain these on tissue papers and serve with deep fried sindhi papad.

You will love these – the savory flavor of the puris along with the spicy papad. Be ready to tingle your taste buds. Serve these hot.

SINGHYUN PATATA
(Drumsticks and Potato Curry)

Singhyun Patata was a loved dish – for the patata!!!! We liked Singhyun too but if we could, we kids would just eat the potatoes from the dish.

But I remember my mother would say to us, "You should eat all vegetables". And, the taste of Singhyun like so many other vegetables, grew on us. The curry used in this recipe especially would taste so good, slightly tangy and a perfect combination with Phulko or even rice.

Our winter meals would include Singhyun because of all its nutrient values and I try to do the same with my family today… Try to ensure a good combination of vegetables, fruit, lentils and legumes so that ours is a healthy diet.

You will love Singhyun Patata – this signature Sindhi dish- for its delectable curry…So let's get to the recipe!

FORTY THREE

Singhyun Patata

🕐 20 MINS   🍽 SERVES 3   👨‍🍳 EASY

INGREDIENTS

Drumsticks (Singhyun) – 2 to 3 (peeled and cut roughly into 3" pieces)

Potato – 1 large (diced into cubes)

Tomatoes – 2 medium sized (puree)

Oil – 2 tbsp

Cumin Seeds – 1 tsp

Curry Leaves – 6 to 7

Hing – ¼ tsp

Ginger (grated) – 1 tsp

Turmeric Powder – ¼ tsp

Coriander Powder – 1 tsp

Red Chili Powder – ½ tsp

Mango Powder – ½ tsp

Green Chili – 1 or 2 (slit length-wise)

Jaggery – 1 tbsp (optional)

Water – 2 cups (or as required)

Salt – as per taste

Garam Masala – 1 tsp

Coriander Leaves – for garnish (finely chopped)

Step 1: Heat oil on medium flame in a pressure cooker. Add cumin seeds; when they crackle add hing, ginger, curry leaves and the tomato puree.

Step 2: Add the spices – turmeric, chili, coriander, mango powder and salt. Stir the mixture and let it cook for some time. Then add the green chili.

Step 3: Add the diced potatoes and singhyun (drumsticks) and stir them into the mixture. Add the water and adjust the consistency.

Step 4: To give the curry that sweet and tangy flavor, add jaggery. This is optional. Mix well, close the pressure cooker, and on high flame cook the drumsticks and potatoes for 3 to 4 whistles or until they are soft and completely cooked.

Step 5: Switch off the flame after the required number of whistles and open the lid only once the cooker naturally depressurizes. Once the vegetables are cooked, mash a few pieces of potatoes to give the curry some texture. Add water if required to adjust the consistency.

Garnish with Garam Masala and finely chopped fresh coriander leaves.

Serve Singhyun Patata at lunch with Phulko or rice.

MITHA CHANWAR / TAHIRI
(Sweet Rice)

At home, Mitha Chanwar (Sweet Rice) were made during Cheti Chand. My grandfather would like Mitha Chanwar and especially on this day, my mother would make Mitha Chanwar and Sai Bhaji for all of us. While as kids we often wondered why rice ought to be sweet especially if we are eating it with Sai Bhaji, but now we love this special day combination!

Cheti Chand is celebrated as New Year's Day for Sindhis and as a commemoration of the birthday of our Saint Jhulelal. Where we lived, 'Cheti Chand jo Melo' (Cheti Chand Fair) would be organized every year at nearby school grounds by the Sindhu Sabha and my father would insist that we go with him. It used to be a cultural evening with Sindhi artists and a number of food stalls serving delicious Sindhi food.

I remember the 'Aarti' (religious ritual of worship) and the traditional Sindhi 'Palav Payan' (Palav literally means the ends of a saree or dupatta/stole) where we would stand holding the ends of our sarees or stoles or shirts or handkerchiefs, with our heads covered, bowing in veneration to receive Jhulelal's blessings. The holy water from the Aarti, would be sprinkled across the crowds, all of us waiting for some drops to fall in our 'Palav' which would be akin to receiving Uderolal's (another name for our Saint) blessings.

After this, small quantities of Mitha Chanwar (sweet rice) would be distributed in pieces of paper to all us devotees. And we kids would be happy to get this Prasad (holy offering) so that we could then run and head straight to the stalls which had all the delicious food!!!

Today I make Mitha Chanwar along with Sai Bhaji on the special day of Cheti Chand and simply love this unique combination.

FORTY FOUR

Mitha Chanwar

30 MINS   SERVES 3   EASY

INGREDIENTS

Rice – 1 cup

Water (to cook rice) – 2 cups

Ghee – 1 tbsp

Salt – A pinch

Dried Dates – 2 (chopped finely)

Cashew Nuts – 8 to 10 (chopped)

Pistachios– 8 to 10 (chopped)

Dried Coconut (Doonghi) – (5 to 6 pieces)

Fennel Seeds – ½ tsp

Black Raisins – 8 to 10

Saffron Strands (optional) - A few soaked in milk

Green Cardamom – 1

FOR SUGAR SYRUP

Sugar – ¾ cup

Water – ½ cup

Step 1: Soak the rice in water for at least 30 minutes before starting to make this dish. If possible, use long grained Basmati variety.

Step 2: In a heavy bottom pan, on medium heat, first heat the ghee and lightly fry the fennel seeds, cashewnuts, pistachios, dried coconut, and raisins.

Step 3: Add the water (water should be double the quantity of rice) and let it come to a boil. Now add the soaked rice.

Step 4: When the rice starts boiling, add a pinch of salt and the cardamom. Cover the pan and cook on low flame.

Step 5: In a separate pan boil the water and sugar to make a light sugar syrup. The sugar syrup must feel like honey or oil when you rub a drop between the tips of your index finger and thumb.

Step 6: Check the rice. If there is no more water and the rice is dry, add the milk soaked saffron. Next, add the sugar syrup, mix and cover the pan for another few minutes.

Note - Instead of making a sugar syrup, you could also just add the sugar into the rice after adding the saffron strands.

Serve Tahiri with Sai Bhaji for an authentic Sindhi meal. Make it for your loved ones on any day and not just the Cheti Chand celebration!

DAL MOONG
(Lentils snack)

Dal Moong as the name suggests has Dal – Bengal Gram and Moong, which is the whole green gram. This combined with boiled vegetables and eaten with Koki (kare mirchan wari) is a treat to behold and taste!

I don't remember eating this as a kid but, I make this often nowadays as it is loved and enjoyed by my family.

FORTY FIVE

Dal Moong

🕐 35 MINS   🍴 SERVES 2   👨‍🍳 MEDIUM

INGREDIENTS

Bengal Gram Lentils – ¼ cup

Whole Green Gram Lentils – ¼ cup

Water – to cook the lentils

Salt – as per taste

Turmeric Powder – ¼ tsp

Coriander Powder – ½ tsp

Mango Powder – ¼ tsp

Chili Powder – ¼ tsp

Roasted Cumin Powder – ¼ tsp

Garam Masala – to sprinkle

FOR TEMPERING

Dry Red Chili – 1

Whole Cumin Seeds – ½ tsp

Oil – 1.5 tbsp

FOR SERVING AND GARNISH

Potato – 1 medium sized (boiled and peeled)

Onions – 1 medium sized (finely chopped)

Date-Tamarind Chutney – 2 tbsp

Coriander Leaves – (finely chopped)

Step 1: Wash and soak the Bengal gram lentils for at least ? to 4 hours. The whole green gram lentils must be soaked longe preferably overnight.

Step 2: In a pressure cooker, add the lentils with enough water. Ad some salt and turmeric powder. Cook the lentils for 5 to 6 whistles o until the lentils are completely cooked. Open the pressure cooker li when it depressurizes naturally.

Step 3: Check the lentils. If they are cooked, mash and whisk them up Take the dal moong out in a serving bowl. Sprinkle the spices – re chili, mango, roasted cumin and coriander powders. Also, sprinkl the garam masala.

Step 4: In a separate smaller pan, prepare the tempering for da moong by heating the oil. When the oil is hot, add the red drie chili and cumin seeds. When they crackle, pour this tempering on th spices sprinkled over the dal moong. Dal moong is ready. Adjust sal

Step 5: Now in a pan, heat some oil. Cut the boiled potatoes in roun shape of ½ inch thickness and shallow fry them till they are lightl browned and crispy.

Step 6: To serve, first plate the potato pieces (you could also us other boiled vegetables like beetroot), then pour spoonfuls of the da moong. Next garnish with the date and tamarind chutney, choppe onions and coriander leaves.

Serve dal moong with Koki (kare mirchan wari). You could also add pieces of finely chopped tomatoes and raw mango as garnish.

MEHAN JI BHAJI
(Apple Gourd Preparation)

Meha (Apple Gourd) is yet another gourd, which is very healthy and makes a great dish. There are many ways to make the Meha, one of which is exactly as the recipe of 'Turi ji bhaji' (though Apple Gourd is a curry and therefore not completely dry like Turi ji Bhaji), but the one I like and make often is stuffed Meha.

My mother mostly made the one with the curry but the stuffed Meha that I make is a nice variation. The stuffing is like the one in the Bharyal Karela recipe and this, used in Meha, tastes and looks delicious.

I serve this with Phulko.

FORTY SIX

Mehan ji Bhaji

⏱ 30 MINS   🍴 SERVES 3   👨‍🍳 MEDIUM

INGREDIENTS

Apple Gourd – 2 medium sized

Potatoes – 1 (peel and cut in round ½ inch thickness shape)

Garlic – 8-10 cloves

Coriander Leaves – ½ cup

Green Chilis – 2 -3

Cumin Seeds – ½ tsp

Turmeric Powder – ¼ tsp

Coriander Powder – ½ tsp

Mango Powder – ½ tsp

Salt – as per taste

Oil – 1 ½ tbsp

Water – ¼ cup

Step 1: For the stuffing, using a mortar pestle, coarsely grind cumin seeds, green chilis, garlic cloves and coriander leaves.

Step 2: In this coarsely ground mixture, add salt, turmeric, coriander and mango powders. The stuffing mixture is ready.

Step 3: Wash and peel the Meha. Then slit them in a X shape for the stuffing. Take care not to slice the Meha. Take small portions of the stuffing and fill in the X shaped slits. Save some for the potatoes and apply the stuffing on to them.

Step 4: In a pressure cooker (you could also use a pan), heat some oil on medium flame. Put the stuffed apple gourds and potatoes and the left over stuffing. Optionally you could also add some finely chopped pieces of tomatoes.

Step 5: Add the water and close the lid. Cook the Meha and potatoes for 5 to 6 whistles or until the Meha are completely cooked.

Serve at meal time with Phulko and some yoghurt.

CHAUNRA
(Black eyed Beans)

Black-eyed beans are a Sindhi favorite. Their nutty earthy flavor, soft and firm texture make them a very nice addition to any meal.

Besides, they are easy to cook and loved by everyone!

My mother made Chaunra often at lunch and I remember eating them with plain rice though nowadays we prefer them with Phulko.

Not just the curry, Chaunra – just boiled with a few spices, taste flavorful and are often used as Prasad (holy offering) during holy events or Pujas (religious ceremony).

Make Chaunra in this Sindhi style and enjoy!

FORTY SEVEN

Chaunra

30 MINS   SERVES 2   EASY

INGREDIENTS

Black Eyed Beans – ½ cup

Onion – 1 medium sized (finely chopped)

Tomatoes – 1 medium sized (finely chopped)

Garlic – 2 to 3 cloves (crushed)

Green Chili – 1 (finely chopped)

Turmeric Powder – ¼ tsp

Coriander Powder – ½ tsp

Salt – as per taste

Oil – 2 tbsp

Coriander Leaves – for garnish (finely chopped)

Water – 1 cup

Step 1: Wash and soak the black eyed beans for 30 minutes.

Step 2: In a pressure cooker, heat oil, on medium flame and add the onions, garlic and green chili. Saute until the onions are a light golden brown. At this time, add the tomatoes and the spices – turmeric and coriander powders and salt.

Step 3: Saute until the tomatoes turn mushy and the mixture release oil. Add the washed and soaked black eyed beans and stir them in the mixture for some time.

Step 4: Add water. Do not add a lot of water as that will make the consistency of the curry runny. Add only enough water such that barely cover the beans.

Step 5: Close the lid of the pressure cooker and cook the beans for to 7 whistles on high flame; switch off the flame once they are cooked completely.

Step 6: Open the lid of the cooker once it has depressurized naturally Mash the beans a little so that the curry looks thick and all together.

Garnish with finely chopped fresh coriander leaves.

Serve warm with Phulko at lunch and a side of yoghurt.

GOBI PATATA
(Cauliflower and Potatoes)

Such a popular dish this one! And so many styles to make this in all of our cuisines…Gobi Patata in the Sindhi cuisine is a very likeable dish and easy to prepare.

We make this dish in so many different ways at home – with dry spices, with yoghurt, in curry, as fritters. But, this recipe is the best. Caramelized onions, tomatoes and the mild flavor of garlic and garam masala…

Enjoy this flavorful dish with Phulko and some yoghurt.

FORTY EIGHT

Gobi Patata

30 MINS   SERVES 2   EASY

INGREDIENTS

Cauliflower - A cup of the florets

Potatoes – 1 medium sized (chopped lengthwise)

Onions – 1 medium sized (finely chopped)

Tomatoes – 1 medium sized (finely chopped)

Garlic – 2 to 3 cloves (crushed)

Ginger – 1 inch (grated)

Chili – 1 finely chopped

Turmeric Powder – ¼ tsp

Red Chili Powder – ¼ tsp

Coriander Powder – ½ tsp

Salt – as per taste

Lemon Juice – for garnish

Homemade Garam Masala – for garnish

Coriander Leaves – for garnish

Oil – 5 to 6 tbsp

Step 1: In a heavy bottom pan, heat about 4 tbsp of oil on medium heat and first shallow fry the cauliflower florets and then the potato pieces. Keep aside.

Step 2: Add some more oil if required and first sauté the onions on medium heat. Add garlic, ginger and chili.

Step 3: When the onions turn translucent, add the shallow fried cauliflower florets and potatoes. Sauté this well for a few minutes. Add salt, turmeric, coriander, red chili powder and sauté, cover and cook.

Step 4: Next, add the tomatoes and sauté well. Cover and cook on low flame until the vegetables are cooked completely.

Step 5: Garnish with a little lemon juice, fresh coriander leaves and sprinkle some homemade garam masala on this beautiful dish!

Serve warm with Phulko and a side of yoghurt at your meal time.

SURAN JO KEEMO
(Elephant Yam Mince)

In the popular hindi movie 'Bawarchi', there is a scene where 'Suran Kebabs' are mistaken for 'Mutton Kebabs'! Such is the texture and taste of the humble Elephant Yam that it is believed to resemble meat!

We eat 'Suran Jo Keemo' with Pav (Buns) because it reminds me of the famous Irani restaurant in Mumbai that serves 'Keema Pav' (Mince Meat with Bread Buns). I am strictly vegetarian and so I like to camouflage this veggie and serve it to my husband and son who are meat lovers!

At home, I remember that my mother would fry these just like the recipe that I have published here for (Taryal Bhee). Boil the yam, press it between your palms (like Tuk) and then deep-fry these in hot oil. Drain and sprinkle the spices (red chili, coriander and mango powders) and salt. They taste yummy and we would love these 'Suran Tuks' with Khichreen or Sindhi Kadhi.

This Keemo recipe is what I make with our regular Sindhi Onion-Tomato mixture and it tastes wonderful. You can also add green peas to the recipe.

You could make either of these two recipes with Suran – Keemo or Tuk – and make your family and friends very happy!

FORTY NINE

Suran jo Keemo

30 MINS   SERVES 3   MEDIUM

INGREDIENTS

Yam – 250 gms

Onion – 1 medium sized (finely chopped)

Tomato – 1 medium sized (finely chopped)

Garlic – 2 to 3 cloves (crushed)

Turmeric Powder – ¼ tsp

Red Chili Powder – ¼ tsp

Coriander Powder – ½ tsp

Bay Leaves - 2

Oil – 1 tbsp

Blanched Green Peas – ¼ cup (Optional)

Garam Masala – for garnish

Coriander Leaves – for garnish

Step 1: In a pressure cooker, boil the yam with salt and water. Yam should be cooked in about 2 whistles. Then mash the yam once the pressure cooker depressurizes naturally.

Step 2: In a pressure cooker on medium flame, heat the oil. When it is hot, add finely chopped onions. Onions should turn into a nice brown color before adding the tomato and the crushed garlic cloves.

Step 2: When the tomatoes turn mushy, add the spices – turmeric, coriander and red chili powders – and salt. Mix well and continue to sauté until the onion-tomato mixture comes together and releases oil.

Step 3: Now add some water, close the pressure cooker and on high flame cook this mixture for about 2 to 3 whistles.

Step 4: When the pressure cooker depressurizes naturally, open the lid and using a dal or potato masher, mash this mixture well so that everything comes together and looks like one thick sauce.

Step 4: Now add the mashed yam, blanched green peas and bay leaves. Sauté the yam well in the onion-tomato and spice sauce on medium to low flame. Stir, then cover and cook.

Step 5: When the yam has blended well with the onion-tomato mixture, remove it in a serving bowl. Garnish with homemade garam masala and finely chopped coriander leaves.

Serve warm with Pav or with Phulko along with some onion and a lemon wedge.

BHARYAL BHINDYUN AIN PATATA
(Stuffed Okra and Potatoes)

This is a wonderful simple dish, which my Mom served alongside any yellow lentils ('Dal') or with the Sindhi Kadhi. Traditionally, Sindhi Kadhi, Bheendi Patata along with Kheerni (Sabudana Kheer) is the very basic food served to a Brahmin after a traditional Puja (holy event) in a Sindhi Household.

The tanginess in this dish comes from "Aamchur" (Mango Powder) and you will find this ingredient used very often in most Sindhi dry preparations.

I remember, I asked my Maasi (maternal aunt) the recipe of one of her preparations and matter of factly, she said, "Add the regular masalas (spices), but don't forget Ambachur (Mango Powder in Sindhi)"! Served with Roti (Indian wheat bread) and a side of yoghurt and the ubiquitous Papad and you have a complete meal!

Bharyal Bhindyun ain Patata

🕐 25 MINS   🍴 SERVES 4   👨‍🍳 EASY

INGREDIENTS

Okra – 250 gms (washed and patted dry)

Potatoes – 2 small sized (peeled and chopped lengthwise)

Oil – 2 to 3 tbsps

DRY SPICES

Turmeric – ½ tsp

Coriander Powder – 2 tbsp

Chili Powder – 1 tsp

Cumin Powder – 1 tsp

Mango Powder – 2 tsps

Salt – as per taste

Step 1: First slit the okra vertically. Do not slice them into two.

Step 2: In a small bowl, mix all the dry spices including salt. Fill a little of this dry spice mixture in each okra. Spare some of the spice mixture for the potatoes.

Step 3: Heat oil in a pan on medium flame. Add the potatoes and sauté with the spice mixture for about 5 to 7 minutes.

Step 4: Next, add the stuffed okra and move it only to ensure that it is roasted on all sides so that the spice mixture stays inside. Cover with a lid, on medium flame and check every few minutes to see if the okra and potatoes are cooked.

This is the basic preparation. However, sometimes, while the okra and potatoes are almost done, I also add cubed onions & tomatoes, cover and cook…all of which is optional but tastes just as good!

Serve hot with rice.

TAMATE JI CHUTNEY
(Tomato Chutney)

What do you make when there are no veggies in the refrigerator and you need to make something that is quick and easy? This Tamate ji Chutney is your answer provided of course you have the staple onions and tomatoes.

Goes well with Phulko or Chanwar, this humble dish also tastes great as salsa to go with your chips or better still the Sindhi papad!!!

This dish would find place on the dinner table sometimes, especially when there were no vegetables or as an accompanying dish to a heavy dal preparation.

We loved it. My father would often ask my mom to prepare "Tamate ji Chutney" so that he could eat with Phulko or Dhodho.

Enjoy this simple dish!

FIFTY ONE

Tamate ji Chutney

20 MINS   SERVES 3   EASY

INGREDIENTS

Onion – 1 small sized

Tomatoes – 2 medium sized

Oil – 1 tbsp

Coriander Powder – ½ tsp

Red Chili Powder – ¼ tsp

Green Chili – 1 finely chopped

Salt – as per taste

Step 1: In a pan, heat the oil and add the finely chopped onions. When they turn translucent (do not brown them), add the finely chopped tomatoes.

Step 2: Add the spices – red chili and coriander powders, finely chopped green chili and salt. Cover and cook on low flame.

Step 3: Open the lid after about 10 minutes and if the tomatoes have turned mushy, using the traditional wooden blender or potato masher, mash the onion tomato mixture so that everything comes together.

Add some water if required and let the mixture cook until it releases oil. Your 'Tamate ji Chutney' is ready. Garnish with some coriander leaves.

Tamate ji Chutney is your ideal side to be eaten warm with Phulka or Dhodho.

SAT BHAJYUN
(7 Vegetables - Diwali Special)

The festival of festivals, this glorious celebration of lights – Diwali, is the most loved and it is only appropriate that I am ending this section with a dish, which is an integral part of our Diwali dinner.

The Sat Bhajyun or 7 vegetables is a wonderful combination of the flavors, the distinct taste and the inherent texture of each vegetable. And really, there are no rules. You can include any vegetables you like; yes there are definitely some favorites!

You can even add them up in your own style - for example, I do not consider the onions or the tomatoes, (which are part of the sauce) as part of the 7 vegetables in this dish! So it is a fun dish and you can experiment. This day is one to celebrate and spend time with family and not one to follow cooking rules!

Every Diwali, my mom served us this dish with Puris after our family 'Lakshmi' (Indian Goddess of wealth) Puja (worship), which would be performed by my Grandfather and Father. All of us would sit around them and follow the rituals; and while these did not take too long, we would wait for the puja to be over so that we could go outside and light the sparklers – first with everyone in the family (called Shagun) and then with all our friends! Oh those were such fun days!

I continue this tradition in my home – of doing the Lakshmi Puja, celebrating with lights, serving sweets and savory to family and friends and then serving "Sat Bhajyun" at dinner.

FIFTY TWO

Sat Bhajyun

⏱ 35 MINS   🍽 SERVES 4   👨‍🍳 MEDIUM

INGREDIENTS

Onion – 1 medium sized (grated or chopped)

Tomatoes – 2 tomatoes (pureed)

Ginger-Garlic Paste – 1 tsp

Spinach – a handful

Fenugreek Leaves – ¼ cup

Coriander Leaves – ¼ cup

Oil – 2 tbsp

The vegetables – Here is where you can choose the ones you want, but for this recipe, I have used lotus root, potatoes, carrots, eggplant, bell pepper/capsicum, green peas and cauliflower. I have used each vegetable in very small quantity to ensure that the flavor of one does not overpower the other.

Turmeric Powder – ¼ tsp

Coriander Powder – 1 tsp

Red Chili Powder – ½ tsp

Garam Masala – ¼ tsp for garnish

Step 1: If using Lotus Root, clean, wash thoroughly, cut to a slant, pieces of about ½ inch thickness and boil in a pressure cooker until cooked completely. If using eggplant/okra, shallow fry them first. If using bell pepper, add it when the dish is almost ready so that it has some time to cook and yet stay a little crunchy.

Step 2: Parboil all the other vegetables – Potatoes, Green Peas, Carrots, Cauliflower florets. Let them be in boiling water for about 5 minutes and then drain them out.

Note- Now the gravy or sauce; you can choose to make the sauce in many different ways. Any one from the Wadi Patata or Gobi Patata or Peas ain Paneer or Kadu-a-ja Kofta recipes will work just fine.

Step 4: In a heavy bottom pan, heat the oil on medium flame; first add grated onion, and ginger garlic paste. Sauté well until the onions turn a golden brown.

Step 5: Blend the spinach, fenugreek (Methi) and coriander leaves in the grinder using some water and add that to the browned onions. Sauté this puree for 4 to 5 minutes on medium flame but keep stirring.

Step 6: Add the tomato puree and the spices – turmeric, chili and coriander powders – and salt. Sauté this onion-tomato mixture until tomatoes have turned soft and the mixture releases oil. Then add water to adjust consistency and let the mixture come to a boil.

Step 7: Now add the vegetables one by one, cover and cook so that the vegetables absorb all the flavors. Do not mix too much. The vegetables should not turn into mush.

Step 8: Once the vegetables have soaked in the flavors and the consistency of the dish is fine, switch off the flame. Take the vegetables out in a bowl, garnish with Garam Masala and coriander leaves.

Happy Diwali!

Side

Indian meals are incomplete without sides. It could be a simple pickle (khatairn) or an elaborate fried preparation (tuks) or just the yoghurt or Buttermilk (Dudh or Matho)!

Sindhi cuisine abounds in Tuks (our twice fried delectable potaoes, Taro, yam) or our fried eggplant or even bitter gourd. And of course the fried bitter gourd peels make such a tasty side to a simple meal.

SANDHYAL BASAR/ BASAR JI KHATAIRN
(Onion Pickle)

We had white ceramic 'Barniyun' (jars) of various sizes with a light brown lid. All pickles would be stored in these. In the summers, my grandmothers together with my mother would make different kinds of khatairn/pickles, but I think the most eaten one would be Sandhyal Basar. It would make a simple dal sumptuous and a simple khichdi taste divine.

This Sindhi pickle is also very healthy because it uses no oil and can be made with many vegetables. We made them with Shallots, Carrots and even Cauliflower. These are also very easy to make - just a few ingredients, and the Khatairn/Pickle is ready.

Today, I mostly make Sandhyal Basar and pair it with a simple dal or khichdi when I am too busy to cook anything else.

FIFTY THREE

Sandhyal Basar

⏱ 15 MINS   🍽 SERVES 6   👨‍🍳 EASY

INGREDIENTS

Shallots – 5 to 6

Yellow Mustard Seeds – 1 tsp

Salt – ¼ tsp

Vinegar – ¼ cup

Water – ½ cup

Green Chilis – 2

Green Garlic – 2 to 3 with the stalks (If not available use 2 to 3 cloves of crushed garlic)

Step 1: First peel, wash and completely dry the shallots and make X shaped slits on the top using your knife. Keep aside.

Step 2: In a mortar-pestle, add the mustard seeds and salt and coarsely pound these. If you have them, add the fresh garlic too along with the stalks. If not just add the garlic cloves and crush.

Step 3: In an airtight jar or Barni, first half the water and vinegar, drop the shallots gently. Then cover the shallots with the rest of the vinegar and water. The shallots should be completely immersed in the water and vinegar.

Step 4: Add the coarsely ground mustard seeds and crushed garlic. Adjust the salt.

Step 5: Next, just break the green chilis into two halves and add them in the jar. Close the lid and now leave the jar in sunlight or a warm place for at least 2 to 3 days.

Step 6: Once the shallots are pickled, keep the jar refrigerated so that the pickle can last longer. You can also leave it out but then they will last for about 7 days.

Enjoy this simple and healthy pickle with any simple meal.

TUK PATATA/ALOO TUK

These double fried potatoes are yummy, crispy and taste best with Kadhi Chanwar or Sai Bhaji or any Dal. My mother made tuk with both potatoes and taro (Kachalu in Sindhi) and both these vegetables have never tasted so good.

Yes, every one fries potatoes but Tuk Patata are unique. They are crispy on the outside, soft on the inside and the hot and tangy flavors from the spices will have you wanting for more.

Tuk Patata would always vanish from the table because everyone in the family loved them so much.

Today I serve Tuk Patata with Kadhi Chanwar or Sai Bhaji. Enjoy this mouth-watering dish!

FIFTY FOUR

Tuk Patata

30 MINS   SERVES 3   MEDIUM

INGREDIENTS

Potatoes – 3 medium sized (peeled)

Oil – to fry

Red Chili Powder – ½ tsp

Coriander Powder – 1 tsp

Mango Powder – ½ tsp

Salt – as per taste

Step 1: Cut the potatoes in a round shape, pieces of at least 1.5 inch in thickness. On both sides make cross shaped slits. Sprinkle salt on these potatoes and leave them aside for at least 15 to 20 minutes. The salt will help in tenderizing the potatoes.

Step 2: After 20 minutes, thoroughly wash the potatoes to get rid of any excess salt, drain and wipe completely dry.

Step 3: Next heat oil and deep-fry these potatoes pieces in hot oil for about 2 to 3 minutes. Next, cover the frying pan and let the potatoes fry on medium for another 2 to 3 minutes. Then take them out and drain on a kitchen towel.

Step 4: When they have cooled a little, press them with the palm of your hand gently, take care not to break them, and deep-fry them once again in hot oil till they turn golden brown and crispy.

Step 5: Sprinkle salt and the spices (chili, coriander and mango powders) and mix well.

Serve hot with Kadhi Chanwar, Sai Bhaji or any other preparation, or eat them just like that!

KARELE JI KATT
(Fried Bitter Gourd Peels)

Karele ji Katt are the crispy, deep – fried peels of the karela, which taste absolutely yummy as a side! Made from what would otherwise be discarded while making karela, we used to eat these crunchy pieces with Phulko and just love them. The rest of the karela, we kids did not really care for, until we grew up!

Make 'Karele ji Katt' with Khichreen or with any other Rice and Dal preparation and enjoy!

FIFTY FIVE

Karele ji Katt

🕐 25 MINS   🍽 SERVES 2   👨‍🍳 EASY

INGREDIENTS

Bitter Gourd Peels – 1 cup (cut lengthwise)

Wheat Flour – 1 tbsp

Yoghurt – 1 tbsp

Salt – ½ tsp

Red Chili Powder – ¼ tsp

Mango Powder – ¼ tsp

Coriander Powder – ½ tsp

Step 1: Mix the ingredients (wheat flour, yoghurt and salt) and rub the peels well. Keep aside for at least an hour.

Step 2: Wash the peels thoroughly and squeeze out all the water.

Step 3: Deep-fry these in hot oil until they are crisp and crunchy. Drain on a kitchen towel.

Sprinkle all the spices – red chili, coriander and mango powders.

Serve these hot with Khichreen or like me eat these with Phulko!

TARYAL WANGARN
(Fried Eggplant)

Taryal Wangarn is a delicious side often served with Khichreen or any Dal and Rice. Very easy to make, deep-fried with some spices. Let's get straight to the recipe.

FIFTY SIX

Taryal Wangarn

🕐 15 MINS   🍽 SERVES 2   👨‍🍳 EASY

INGREDIENTS

Eggplant – 1 small

Red Chili Powder – ½ tsp

Coriander Powder – ½ tsp

Mango Powder – ¼ tsp

Salt – as per taste

Step 1: Cut the eggplants into thin slices of round shape about ½ to ¾ inch thickness and make X shaped slit on each slice.

Step 2: In a vessel, pour some water and salt. Dip the eggplant pieces in the salt water for at least 10 to 15 minutes.

Step 2: Deep-fry the slices until they turn light golden brown. Drain them on a kitchen towel and sprinkle all the spices – red chili, coriander, mango powder and salt.

You could also shallow fry the eggplant. For this, in a pan, heat about 3 to 4 tablespoons of oil. Add the eggplant pieces and shallow fry until they are a golden brown in color. Sprinkle salt and all the spices on top of the eggplant pieces. Serve hot.

Serve hot with Khichreen or with any simple Dal and Chanwar meal.

TARYAL KARELO
(Fried Bitter Gourd)

Taryal Karelo is a nice side just like Taryal Wangarn. Goes well with any Dal and Chanwar combination or with Phulko.

I love to eat this with Phulko, no bhaji, no dal. Just Phulko and taryal karelo tastes so good; for me, it's a complete meal!

Lets get to the recipe.

Taryal Karelo

🕐 15 MINS   🍽 SERVES 3   👨‍🍳 EASY

INGREDIENTS

Bitter Gourd (Karela) – 2 medium sized

Oil – to deep fry

Salt – 1 tbsp

Red Chili Powder – ¼ tsp

Coriander Powder – ½ tsp

Mango Powder – ¼ tsp

Step 1: Peel the Karela (make Karele ji Katt with the peels!), cut into round thinly sliced pieces. Rub salt on them and set aside for at least 30 minutes. This will make them soft and will take away some of the bitterness.

Step 2: Wash thoroughly and dry on a kitchen towel. Heat oil in a pan and deep-fry the dried pieces until they turn golden brown.

Step 3: Drain them on a kitchen towel. Sprinkle red chili, coriander and mango powders.

Serve hot with Khichreen or as a side to any meal.

KACHALU TUK
(Taro Root Fry)

We love these twice-fried tuks – be it potato or taro root. A perfect side to any meal, these taste so good that we would like these to be the main meal itself…not possible – they are deep fried and two times at that! I think we Sindhis truly like our twice-fried food! Remember sanna pakoras?

As a child, I got confused between Aaloo (Potato) tuk and Kachalu (Taro root) tuk. I could not make out the difference and I used to tell my mom that they taste the same. Now when I hear my son and husband saying the same thing, I am not sure whether I should be happy or sad!

I think Kachalu has its own distinct taste and while we eat it as a bhaji too, nothing compares to Kachalu twice fried…in the inimitable Sindhi way!

FIFTY EIGHT

Kachalu Tuk

⏱ 30 MINS   🍽 SERVES 4   👨‍🍳 MEDIUM

INGREDIENTS

Kachalu (Taro Root) – 7 to 8 (for Tuk, always buy small oblong shaped thin Taro Root).

Water – to cook

Oil – to deep-fry

Salt – as per taste

Red Chili Powder – ½ tsp

Coriander Powder – 2 tsp

Mango Powder – 1 tsp

Step 1: In a pressure cooker, boil the taro roots with enough water and salt, on high flame for at least 2 to 3 whistles or until the roots are cooked.

Step 2: Open the lid when the cooker naturally depressurizes, take the taro roots out, let them cool for some time and then peel. Meanwhile, in a bowl, combine the dry spices – red chili, coriander and mango powders – and salt. Keep aside.

Step 3: In a pan, heat oil on high flame and when it is smoking hot, slowly and carefully slide the cooked and peeled taro roots. Fry them until they are a light golden brown, then take them out and strain on a kitchen towel.

Step 4: When they have cooled and you are able to handle them, with a knife, make a vertical slit in each of them taking care that you do not slice them into two.

Step 5: Fill the slits with the dry spice mix prepared in step 2. (Save some to sprinkle on top after they are fried.) Now press the taro root between your palms so that the spices are sealed between the two pieces.

Step 6: Once again, heat the oil on high flame and when it is smoking hot, slide these pressed taro roots and fry until golden brown on both sides. Then drain on kitchen towel, sprinkle the dry spices and serve.

Serve warm with Khichreen or as a side to your meals.

TARYAL BHEE
(Fried Lotus Roots)

Bhee occupies a very special place in the Sindhi cuisine and it turns up in so many ways! Taryal Bhee is a very common side and you will find it often at our wedding menus and well, also in any Sindhi household!

Taryal Bhee goes great with Sindhi Khichreen, or any Dal and Chanwar.

Very easy to make, after of course you have cleaned the Lotus Root of all the mud, washed it thoroughly and cut the pieces to a slant!

126

FIFTY NINE

Taryal Bhee

30 MINS   SERVES 3   EASY

INGREDIENTS

Bhee (Lotus Root) Pieces – ½ inch thick cut to a slant

Oil – to deep Fry

Salt – as per taste

Red Chili Powder – ½ tsp

Mango Powder – ¼ tsp

Step 1: Boil the Bhee pieces in a pressure cooker with water and enough salt. Cook for about 3 to 4 whistles or until the Bhee pieces are completely cooked (if the Bhee is fresh, it will take lesser number of whistles to cook so check accordingly).

Step 2: Open the lid of the cooker once it depressurizes naturally and strain the water from the Bhee pieces.

Step 3: In a pan, heat oil on medium flame. Deep-fry the Bhee pieces until they turn golden brown and crispy. Add salt if required. Sprinkle red chili, cumin, coriander and mango powders and serve.

Serve warm with Khichreen or as a side to your meals.

MATHO
(Buttermilk)

Matho is made often in summers but especially during Thadri. Along with Lola, Besani and other delicacies, Matho is such a great combination.

Matho is delicious and not just buttermilk. It has gram flour dumplings (boondi) and spices that make it both a refreshing and healthy drink.

And you can drink it whenever you like and not just at Thadri! At home, we made it often but on Thadri day, there would definitely be boondi inside and we would love to slurp Matho making a nice white moustache on our mouths!

SIXTY

Matho

15 MINS   SERVES 2   EASY

INGREDIENTS

Yoghurt (preferably homemade) – ½ cup

Water – 1 ½ cup

Salt – as per taste

FOR TEMPERING

Ghee – ½ tsp

Asafoetida – a pinch

Mustard Seeds – ½ tsp

Curry Leaves – 3 to 4

FOR MAKING BOONDI

Gram Flour – ½ cup

Water – ½ cup

Salt – ¼ tsp

Step 1: For the Boondi make a smooth, lump free, thick batter using gram flour, salt and water. Whisk for at least 5 minutes so that it becomes soft and fluffy. In a pan on medium flame, heat oil and drop the batter through frying spoon that has small holes so that the droplets fall into the oil. Fry until the droplets (Boondi) float on top. Remove and drain on kitchen towel.

Step 2: Save some of the crispy boondi for garnish. Soften rest of the Boondi by dropping them in warm water. When they soften after about 15 to 20 minutes, drain them and keep aside.

Step 3: In a vessel, whisk the yoghurt until it is lump free and add water. You can increase the water quantity to this buttermilk depending on the desired consistency. Add salt to taste.

Step 4: Heat ghee in a small pan and when it is hot, add asafoetida (hing), mustard seeds and curry leaves. When mustard seeds crackle, pour this tempering on to the prepared buttermilk.

Step 5: Add the softened boondi into the buttermilk. Chill and serve in glasses. Garnish with the saved crispy boondi.

Serve chilled during Thadri festival or at your summertime meals.

Snack

Sindhi snacks sometimes can be a full meal, Dal, Chola Dabal or even the Dal Toast for example! The use of bread (dabal)/pav, in our snack preparations is quite unique and special.

Pakoras or Tikkis truly make for our comfort food and we love to indulge in these, especially when it is raining outside and we can sit indoors with a hot cup of tea!

SANNA PAKORA
(Gram flour and Onion Fritters)

This is an iconic Sindhi snack that is almost always made for our guests. Served with ketchup or green chutney these taste delightful.

Lucky us, we ate them every Monday of the week at dinner. It was a ritual; my Mother made this, very light to the stomach, petite yellow lentils (moong dal), sanna pakoras and of course phulka/rotis every Monday dinner.

We would wait at dinnertime and knowingly ask my Mother, "What have you made today Mommy?" And she would smile and say "Pal Dakora!" The first time we were completely confused until my brother got it and clapping his hands said "Dal Pakora". We were so happy!

While different kind of pakoras are so common in India, Sanna Pakora are made a little differently, which is probably the secret of their crispiness. I believe they are called Sanna because of their small size. (Sanna in Sindhi means thin.)

SIXTY ONE

Sanna Pakora

⏱ 20 MINS   🍴 SERVES 4   👨‍🍳 EASY

INGREDIENTS

Onion – 1 medium sized

Gram Flour (Besan) – 1 cup

Water – to make a thick batter

Green Chilis – 1 (finely chopped)

Coriander Leaves – a few (finely chopped)

Oil – to deep fry

Step 1: First mix the chopped onion and the gram flour. Add water slowly to make a thick lump free batter which falls like ribbons. Now to this add finely chopped chili, coriander leaves and salt. Add a tablespoon of oil to the batter.

Step 2: Now in medium hot oil, add ladles full of the batter and fry these big-sized pakoras or fritters till they are half done. Drain them out on tissue paper and let them cool a little.

Step 3: Now break each half-done pakora or fritter into smaller pakoras (each big-sized pakora or fritter can be broken into 4-5 sanna pakoras) and deep fry them in hot oil till they are golden brown and crisp.

Serve hot with ketchup or chutney or like us have them at dinner!!!

ALOO TIKKI
(Potato Pattie)

Oh how we absolutely love Aloo ji Tikki! Whether it is with Sai Bhaji-Chanwar or with Sindhi Kadhi or with our favorite combination – Chola (Chick Peas) or just like that.

Aloo ji Tikki or Aloo Tikki until today is a 'must-have' at all our birthday celebrations! Along with Chola and Dabal (Bread) and the customary cake. Of course, when we were kids, my mom would have made Kada Prasad and got it blessed at the Gurudwara in the morning, but in the evening, the celebration would include Chola Dabal and Aloo Tikki.

We loved our birthdays because of this yummy combination. Our cousins would come over too and we would be playing, and enjoying until it was time to go to bed so we would be in time for school the next day!

This Aloo Tikki recipe is the most basic one and we sometimes also make 'Aloo ji Chap' which is heart shaped and stuffed with Chana Dal (Bengal Gram).

As I write this recipe, I am flooded with memories from our birthday celebrations, the laughter, the love, the singing and the fun. Here's to all your celebrations too!

SIXTY TWO

Aloo Tikki

30 MINS   10 PIECES   MEDIUM

INGREDIENTS

Boiled Potatoes – 2 to 3 medium sized

Bread Slices – 3 to 4

Cumin Seeds – ½ tsp

Green Chilis – 2

Coriander Leaves – ¼ cup (finely chopped)

Salt – as per taste

Step 1: Peel the potatoes and mash them with light hands. Next, dip the bread slices in water, immediately squeeze the water out and add to the mashed potatoes.

Step 2: Add finely chopped green chilis, cumin seeds, coriander leaves and salt. Mix well; apply a little oil on your palms. Take small portions of the potato mix and make round shaped 'tikkis'.

Step 3: Heat oil in a heavy bottomed frying pan and on high flame, deep-fry the tikkis until they are golden brown on both sides. Drain them on a kitchen towel.

Note – I always fry one tikki to see whether it has enough bread. If it breaks, it could be because either the oil is not hot enough or the mix needs more bread for binding.

Serve tikki while it is still hot with ketchup, chutney or Chola and our other loved combinations.

TAMATE BASAR JO TOAST
(Tomato and onion stuffed toasted sandwich)

This yummy toast would be our favorite! At a time when there were no fancy toasters or sandwich makers, my mother would make this toast simply on her tawa (iron griddle) that she would also use for making Koki, Phulko, Chillo, Dhodho, Paratho and other breads!

How we would love this crispy toast served with ketchup! Those were the days, when snacking meant homemade healthy food – koki, poha, upma etc.

My best friend from school still calls this the "Sindhi Toast" and sometimes, when she came home we would stand in the kitchen and chat while I made this for the both of us.

Sunday dinner for my father would be tamate basar jo toast for many years because he would want to eat something light on Sundays after the usually heavy lunch.

My mom would occasionally replace tamato and basar with boiled potatoes but that would have to be planned since boiling potatoes would take long. A quick, crispy mouthwatering snack and one for which we three kids were every ready – tamate basar jo toast!

Here's the recipe which is pure nostalgia to this day. Make it on your tawa (iron griddle) for that original, traditional and nostalgic feeling…

SIXTY THREE

Tamate Basar jo Toast

⏱ 20 MINS   🍽 SERVES 2   👨‍🍳 EASY

INGREDIENTS

Bread – 4 slices (for 2 toasts)

Onion – ½ medium sized (very finely chopped)

Tomatoes – 1 medium sized (very finely chopped; without the pulp and seeds)

Green Chili – 1 (finely chopped)

Coriander Leaves – for garnish (finely chopped)

Salt – as per taste

Oil/Butter – 1 tbsp

Step 1: In a vessel, mix the finely chopped onions, tomatoes, chili coriander leaves and salt. Make a sandwich by placing some of this stuffing between 2 bread slices.

Step 2: Heat the griddle and on low flame drizzle some oil or butter Place the sandwich on the heated griddle. Now place a flat steel thal (plate) on top of the sandwich and place something heavy on the thal (plate) to press the sandwich. I usually place a heavy mortar pestle.

Step 3: After a few minutes, check if the side facing the griddle is done. If it has turned brown and crispy, flip it and now toast the other side by drizzling some oil/butter, pressing the side with the plate and the weight.

Step 4: Once both the sides are golden brown and crispy, plate the toast, cut it diagonally and serve with ketchup.

Enjoy this toast at breakfast or as an anytime snack!

TARYAL PHULKO
(Fried wheat flatbread)

Here is yet another easy dish made from left over phulka/rotis. This is an evening snack and tastes great with tea.

Sometimes my mother would just surprise us with this yummy snack in the afternoons when we would have just finished our homework or would have come back after playing in the building compound with our friends. (I remember we would play "Saakhli, Dabba Ice Spice, Dog and the bone, Hopscotch and so many variations of Hide and Seek"!)

Coming back to the recipe, this crispy Taryal Phulko was my mother's go to recipe to satisfy our hungry tummies quickly. There were not so many options those days to snack! At best, there would be Britannia Marie Cookies at home!

Today I make these for my son and he relishes them as much as we did as kids. Some tastes don't change I think!

SIXTY FOUR

Taryal Phulko

⏱ 10 MINS   🍴 SERVES 3   👨‍🍳 EASY

INGREDIENTS

Left over phulka/rotis – 3 to 4

Oil – to deep fry

Sugar – to sprinkle

Step 1: Heat oil in a heavy bottomed pan. Meanwhile cut each phulko/roti into 4 triangles.

Step 2: Deep-fry each piece until it is crispy. Drain on a tissue paper. Sprinkle sugar and serve.

How easy is that? You could also make it savory and fancy by serving with different toppings.

BESAN JO CHILLO
(Gram Flour savory pancake)

Besan jo Chillo is a quick and tasty snack that, we as kids would be treated to, whenever we were ravenously hungry and could not wait until mealtime.

I remember that we would eat Besan jo Chillo with Phulko or a bread slice, but I think it can be eaten just like that too.

Nowadays I make it regularly and relish it at any mealtime. My preferred way is to eat it with Phulko but besan jo chillo between 2 bread slices and some ketchup or chutney makes for great comfort food too!

SIXTY FIVE

Besan jo Chillo

⏱ 30 MINS   🍽 SERVES 4   👨‍🍳 MEDIUM

INGREDIENTS

Gram Flour (Besan) – 1 cup

Onions – 1 medium sized (finely chopped)

Tomatoes – ½ medium sized (finely chopped)

Green Chili – 1 (finely chopped)

Coriander Leaves – a handful (finely chopped)

Salt – as per taste

Water – to make batter

Oil – to make Chillo

Step 1: In a vessel, combine the gram flour and water. Mix it well to make a thick, lump free batter of flowing consistency. Whisk it for some time so that it is very smooth and falls to make ribbons. Let it rest for a few minutes.

Step 2: Meanwhile chop all the ingredients and combine into the batter – onions, tomatoes, chili, coriander leaves and salt.

Step 3: Heat a griddle on medium flame. Then lower the flame, pour a spoonful of the batter and spread it around in a round shape. Increase the flame to medium, drizzle oil around the sides and let the chillo cook. Do not flip until the top of the Chillo has become dry.

Step 4: When the Chillo is cooked, it will leave the pan easily, flip it and cook the other side. When both sides are roasted nicely and the color turns a light golden brown, plate it and serve.

When making the next Chillo, sprinkle some water on the griddle to bring down the temperature; again on low flame, pour the batter, slightly increase the flame when the chillo is cooking and remove it when cooked on both sides. Follow the same procedure when making all the Chillas.

Serve this quick snack with ketchup or green chutney!

BHEE-A-JA PAKORA
(Lotus Root Fritters)

Sindhis love their 'Bhee' and this is evident from all the different Bhee preparations – Bhee Patata, Bhee-a-ja Pakora, Taryal Bhee and many others.

Pakoras are great as a snack and great as a side with any meal. And, when you make Bhee-a-ja Pakora you don't have to worry about the hairy fibres in the Bhee. As kids we would love these pakoras along with Sindhi Kadhi or even just as a snack with some chutney and ketchup.

Nowadays I make these pakoras mostly with Dal and Rice or Khichreen for my family and me to relish!

SIXTY SIX

Bhee-a-ja Pakora

25 MINS　　**SERVES 3**　　**EASY**

INGREDIENTS

Lotus Roots – 10 to 15 (½" slices - always cut lotus root in a slant)

Gram Flour – 1 cup

Water – as required to make batter

Salt – as per taste

Red Chili Powder – ½ tsp

Step 1: In a pressure cooker, on high flame, cook the Bhee slices i[n] water and some salt. Cook them for 3 to 4 whistles or until they are done.

Step 2: When the cooker depressurizes naturally, open the lid and strain the bhee. In the meanwhile, prepare the better using gram flou[r] and water.

Step 3: The batter should be thick and lump free, smooth and o[f] flowing consistency (should fall like ribbons). Whisk nicely so that the batter is fluffy. Add the red chili powder and salt.

Step 4: In a pan heat some oil on medium flame. Now dip the Bhee[e] slice in the batter such that it coated all over and drop it gently int[o] hot oil.

Step 5: Drop all the batter coated Bhee slices into the oil and fry ti[ll] they are golden brown on both sides.

Serve hot with ketchup or as a side to a regular Dal and Chanwa[l] fare or Khichreen.

DAL TOAST/ SANDWICH
(Lentils Toast)

Dal Toast is a delicious snack and a very popular Sindhi street food. Bread does occupy a special place in a Sindhi kitchen. I remember when we ran out of Phulka, we would eat dal with a slice of bread.

I remember my Father eating dal with bread even as a meal. He would pour dal on a slice of bread and then eat with a spoon relishing every bite.

And I do too…I love to eat bread with dal, fried potatoes, sanna pakora, tikki, besan jo chillo and of course Chola!

Dal Toast is a snacky version of just dal poured on bread. There's garnish, chutneys, sev and of course the stuffed toasted sandwich making this a truly desirable dish!

SIXTY SEVEN

Dal Toast

🕐 15 MINS   🍽 SERVES 2   👨‍🍳 EASY

INGREDIENTS

FOR TOAST

Sliced Bread – 2

Boiled Potato – ½

Green Chutney – 1 tsp

Butter – ½ tsp

Salt – as per taste

Pepper – to sprinkle

DAL

Dal Makhni (recipe on page 79) – 1 ladle full

FOR GARNISH

Onions – 1 medium sized (finely chopped)

Date and Jaggery Chutney – 2 tsps

Green Chutney – 2 tsps

Sev (Gram Flour fried noodles) – 2 to 3 tbsps

Lemon Juice – ½ tsp

Coriander Leaves – finely chopped

Chat Masala – to sprinkle

Step 1: Butter one slice of bread and apply chutney on the other slice. Place finely sliced round potato pieces on one side, sprinkle salt and pepper. Place the other slice on top and toast the sandwich (as in Tamate Basar jo Toast) on a griddle. (You could use other vegetables as well instead of potatoes like sliced boiled beetroot, sliced onions, sliced cucumber and others).

Step 2: In a serving plate, place the toast, cut it in diagonally. Then pour a ladle full of Makhni dal, spoons of green and date, tamarind & jaggery chutneys, finely chopped onion and sev. Sprinkle chaat masala, lemon juice and finely chopped coriander leaves.

Serve this unique street food to your loved ones and watch them enjoy every bite!

PATATE JA PAKORA
(Potato Fritters)

Patate ja Pakora are a must have when it is raining outside and you can sit at the window with a warm cup of tea watching the world go by. That is my definition of a perfect afternoon!

At home, we ate these pakoras whenever we felt like eating something crispy and yummy. Yes, the Sanna Pakoras taste delicious too, but they have to be twice fried, bhee has to be boiled for the Bhee-a-ja Pakoras; so the fastest in this category are the potato ones and we love these equally!

Patate ja Pakoras taste great with any Dal and Chanwar combination and by themselves, just with some ketchup, they make such a wonderful combination at tea.

My family loves these fritters; I make them whenever we feel like having pakoras and there is no time to prepare anything else elaborate.

SIXTY EIGHT

Patate ja Pakora

⏱ 30 MINS   🍽 SERVES 3   👨‍🍳 MEDIUM

INGREDIENTS

Potatoes – 2 medium sized

Gram Flour (Besan) – ½ cup

Water as required

Salt – as per taste

Red Chili Powder – ½ tsp

Oil – to deep fry

Step 1: Peel and chop the potatoes in round shape and slice them as thin as possible or at least ¼". Then rub some salt and keep them aside for 10 to 15 minutes.

Step 2: Meanwhile, in a vessel, combine the gram flour and water to make a thick, smooth and lump free batter. It should be of flowing consistency (fall like ribbons) but thick enough to coat the potato slices.

Step 3: Add salt and red chili powder and whisk the batter so that becomes soft and fluffy. Beat in a single direction for at least 2 minutes.

Step 4: Heat oil on medium flame. While the oil heats, wash the potatoes under water thoroughly and dry them on a kitchen towel. Then take each slice, coat it in the gram flour batter and add into the heated oil.

Step 5: Fry all the potato slices, on medium flame, in the same way and take them out when they are golden brown on both sides. Drain them on a kitchen towel and serve hot with ketchup or green chutney.

Serve hot at your tea time or as an anytime snack.

CHAP CHOLA
(Stuffed Potato Pattie with Chickpeas)

Chap Chola is an iconic Sindhi snack especially the heart shaped Chap, filled with Charan ji dal. It is also the Ragda Pattice (popular street food in Mumbai and other cities) equivalent. Chola (chick peas) is sometimes replaced by white peas but use Chola if you want an authentic Sindhi recipe on your plate!

At home, we would buy ready-made Chap from a middle aged man who would come to our house all the way from Ulhasnagar with all Sindhi goodies like Papad, Kheecha, Chap etc…My father would always buy the chap from him along with Papad and Kheecha and he would make it a point to keep a packet or two for his sisters.

The Chap would have to be shallow fried in oil/ghee before serving and we would relish them with Chola and sometimes just with the chutneys. Either ways they tasted great and were a healthier snack since they were never deep-fried.

Chap Chola garnished with chutneys, onions, sev and coriander is a treat to the eyes and the taste buds. The sweet and savory chutneys, the flavorful Chola, the spicy dal filled Chap - just the thought makes me want to dig into a flavorful plate of Chap Chola.

SIXTY NINE

Chap Chola

🕐 30 MINS   🍴 SERVES 3   👨‍🍳 MEDIUM

INGREDIENTS

FOR CHAP

Potatoes – 3 medium sized

Poha (Puffed Rice) – ½ cup

Salt – as per taste

FOR STUFFING

Chana (dal) – Split chickpeas – ½ cup

Salt – as per taste

Turmeric Powder

Cumin Powder – ¼ tsp

Coriander Powder – ½ tsp

Red Chili Powder – ¼ tsp

Mango Powder – ¼ tsp

Lemon Juice – ½ tsp

Coriander Leaves – ¼ cup

Green Chili – 1 finely chopped

Oil – to shallow fry

PREPARE THE POTATOES

Step 1: Boil the potatoes in water. When done, peel mash and keep aside.

Step 2: Grind the poha (puffed rice) into a fine powder. Add this powder to the mashed potatoes.

Note - The amount depends on the quality of potatoes.

Step 3: Keep adding the powdered poha until the potatoes feel dry and do not stick to your hand. Add salt to taste.

PREPARE THE DAL STUFFING

Step 4: First soak the dal for at least 3 hours. In a pressure cooker, boil the dal along with salt and turmeric and water. Add only enough water to barely cover the dal.

Step 5: Cook the dal for about 3 whistles or until it is done. Open the lid once it depressurizes naturally. Do not overcook the dal and do not mash it.

Step 6: Using a strainer, strain all the water from the dal. It should be dry so you can add all the spices and use it as a stuffing.

Step 7: Add all the spices – cumin, coriander, red chili and mango powders. Add the lemon juice, finely chopped green chili and coriander leaves. Add salt if required since it was added when boiling it too.

Step 8: Mix the spices well with the dal. Here, you can add some garam masala and some fennel seeds powder if you like its flavor.

INGREDIENTS

FOR CHOLA

Chick Peas – 1 cup

Tomato – 1 medium sized

Salt – as per taste

Turmeric Powder – ¼ tsp

Cumin Powder – ¼ tsp

Coriander Powder – ½ tsp

Red Chili Powder – ¼ tsp

Chole Masala – ½ tsp

Garam Masala (optional) – ¼ tsp

Coriander Leaves – ¼ cup

Oil – 2 tbsp

Water – as required

MAKING THE CHAP

Usually Chap are heart shaped so I use a heart shaped cookie cutter to shape them. If you do not have a cookie cutter you could just make them round.

Step 9: To make the Chap, first apply some oil on your palms, take a portion of the boiled potatoes and flatten it. Use cookie cutter if using to get the heart shape.

Step 10: Fill in the dal stuffing in the center and close/cover the center with more boiled potato portion. Make the Chaps in this way with all of the mashed potato and the dal stuffing.

Step 11: Roll each Chap in a bowl of the powdered poha. You can also use all purpose flour or corn flour for this step.

Step 12: Heat oil/ghee on a griddle, on medium to low flame and shallow fry each Chap until is a golden brown on both sides.

CHOLA

Step 1: Soak the Chola (Chickpeas) overnight or at least 8 to 9 hours.

Step 2: In a pressure cooker, boil the Chickpeas with salt and about 1.5 cups of water for about 5 to 6 whistles or until they are done.

Step 3: In a heavy bottomed pan, on medium flame, heat oil and add all the dry spices – turmeric, red chili, coriander, cumin powders and chole masala.

Step 4: Saute the dry spices in oil until the raw smell goes away. Sprinkle some water to ensure that the spices don't stick to the pan.

Step 5: Add finely chopped tomatoes to this mixture and cook on medium flame until the tomato and spice mixture releases oil.

Step 6: Add the boiled Chola along with some of the water in which these were boiled and let the Chola simmer on medium flame for at least 25 to 30 minutes so that they absorb all the flavors. Add salt to taste.

Step 7: Add water to adjust consistency, stir and let the Chola simmer for at least another 15 to 20 minutes. Sprinkle Garam Masala if using and finely chopped coriander leaves and switch off the flame.

Step 8: To assemble, first place the Chap on the serving plate, pour Chola on top. Garnish with Green (Coriander and Mint) and Sweet (Date and Jaggery) chutneys, finely chopped onions, sev and finely chopped coriander leaves.

Enjoy this mouthwatering delicacy with your friends and family over cups of tea and loving conversations!

ATTE JO CHILLO
(Wheat flour Pancake)

Atte Jo Chillo is a healthy and hearty breakfast, snack, meal! Like Besan jo Chillo, we ate Atte jo Chillo whenever we were hungry and needed a quick snack to satiate our hungry tummies!

I make it often for myself and I like that it is so healthy and easy to whip up especially when I am busy with numerous deadlines!

Enjoy this chillo with ketchup or green chutney.

SEVENTY

Atte jo Chillo

🕐 30 MINS   🍽 6 PIECES   👨‍🍳 MEDIUM

INGREDIENTS

Wheat Flour – 1 cup

Gram Flour – 1 tbsp

Fine Sooji (Semolina) – 1 tbsp

Onion – 1 small (finely chopped)

Green Chili – 1 (finely chopped)

Coriander Leaves – ¼ cup

Red Chili Powder – ¼ tsp

Salt – as per taste

Water – as required

Oil – 1 tsp per chillo

Step 1: In a vessel combine the flours and add water to make a thick, lump free, smooth batter. Whisk well for some time to incorporate some air. Rest for 15 minutes.

Step 2: Add the rest of the ingredients (except oil) to this batter and mix well. Add water to adjust consistency of the batter. Batter should be thick and smooth.

Step 3: Heat a griddle on medium flame and sprinkle oil over the griddle. Then lower the flame, pour a spoonful of the batter and spread it around in a round shape.

Step 4: Flip the Chillo only when the top of the Chillo has become dry. Roast the Chillo on low flame for some time.

Step 5: Apply a spoonful of oil on the side facing up and flip it. Now increase the flame to medium and let the side roast completely.

Step 6: Next apply a spoonful of oil on the other side facing up, flip it and on medium flame roast this side too.

When both sides are roasted nicely and the color turns a light golden brown, plate it and serve.

When making the next Chillo, sprinkle some water on the griddle to bring down the temperature; again on low flame, pour the batter after greasing the griddle, slightly increase the flame when the chillo is cooking and remove it when cooked on both sides. Follow the same procedure when making all the Chillas.

Serve this quick snack with ketchup or green chutney at your breakfast or tea time!

BATAN/BATAR PAPDI CHAAT
(Savory Snack)

Batan Papdi Chaat is a very popular Sindhi street food. With the 'Batan', spicy and sweet Chutneys and Papdi garnish, this makes for a very flavorful anytime snack and can easily be made at home too!

Batan/Batar as the name suggests is a small hard bread bun. Usually it is dipped in tea before eating; other times maska (Butter and Sweet Cream) is applied before biting into it. Either way, it tastes great with a cup of warm cardamom or ginger tea.

In this Chaat recipe, the Sindhis have taken the everyday Batan to a whole new level, making it the center of this Chaat dish.

Batan Papdi Chaat is a must-have to satiate all your sweet, spicy and flavorful culinary desires!

SEVENTY ONE

Batan Papdi Chaat

25 MINS   SERVES 3   MEDIUM

INGREDIENTS

FOR POTATOES:

Potatoes – 2 boiled, peeled and mashed

Salt – as per taste

Red Chili Powder – ½ tsp

Chaat Masala – ½ tsp

FOR GREEN CHUTNEY:

Coriander Leaves – ½ cup

Green Chili – 2 to 3

Mint Leaves – ½ cup

Spinach – ¼ cup

Cumin Powder – ½ tsp

Lemon Juice – ½ tsp

Tamarind Paste – ½ tsp

Water – ¼ cup

Salt – as per taste

Black Salt – pinch

FOR TAMARIND WATER:

Tamarind – ¼ cup soaked in ½ cup water for at least 20 minutes

Water – 1 cup

Sugar – 1 tsp

Cumin Powder – ½ tsp

Red Chili Powder – ½ tsp

Chaat Masala – ½ tsp

Salt – as per taste

FOR GARNISH:

Onion – 1 medium sized finely chopped

Papdi and Sev

Coriander Leaves – finely chopped

FOR ONE SERVING:

Batan or Batar (Small hard buns) – 3 buns cut in half each

Step 1: Make the green chutney by blending all the ingredients except water. Add the water as required and blend into a smooth paste. Keep refrigerated.

Step 2: For the Tamarind water, first strain the pulp from the tamarind, soaked in water. In a heavy bottom pan, on low flame, heat the tamarind pulp and add at least a cup of water. Add the sugar and cook the tamarind water until the sugar melts. Next, add the cumin and chili powders, chaat masala and salt. Mix well and let the tamarind water come to a boil. Keep aside, cool and refrigerate.

Step 3: To the boiled and mashed potatoes, add red chili powder, chaat masala and salt. Keep aside.

Step 4: To serve, first cut the batans into half horizontally. In the tamarind water, add 2 tablespoons of the green chutney and mix.

Step 5: Soak the batans in the tamarind water for 10 seconds (do not soak longer otherwise the batans will turn soggy). Take them out on a serving plate. Over each batan place some of the mashed potatoes. Then pour a teaspoon of the green chutney on the potatoes. Next, place the finely chopped onions on top of the mashed potaoes on each batan. Garnish all the batan tops with sev crush papdi and sprinkle all over the batans.

Add some more tamarind water all over the batans and garnish with some more sev and papdi before serving.

Enjoy this yummy anytime snack!

BHEE-A-JI TIKKI
(Lotus Root Pattie)

Here is yet another Tikki recipe that is twice fried and uses Lotus Root (Bhee). This quintessential Sindhi snack is loved by all especially kids. With some ketchup, this is a great snack to serve your guests during parties and get-togethers.

SEVENTY TWO

Bhee-a-ji Tikki

⏱ 30 MINS   🍴 6 PIECES   👨‍🍳 MEDIUM

INGREDIENTS

Potato – 1 (boiled and peeled)

Lotus Root – 20 to 25 - 1" pieces (cleaned and boiled)

Gram Flour – 1 cup

Green Chilis – 1 (finely chopped)

Coriander Leaves – ¼ cup (finely chopped)

Mango Powder – ¼ tsp

Coriander Powder – ½ tsp

Oil – A tablespoon for the batter and to fry

Salt – as per taste

Step 1: Mash the boiled potato and lotus root pieces and mix them together.

Step 2: Add salt, green chili, coriander leaves, mango powder and coriander powder to the potato-lotus root mixture. Keep aside.

Step 3: In a vessel, make gram flour batter, by mixing gram flour and water. Add some salt and a tablespoon of oil. The batter should be thick, smooth and lump free. It should fall like ribbons.

Step 4: Make medium sized balls of the potato and lotus root mix, dip them in the gram flour batter such that the balls are coated well and deep-fry them in medium hot oil.

Step 5: After the balls have turn a light golden brown, take them out and drain them on a kitchen towel.

Step 6: Lightly press each ball between your palms and deep fry one more time in hot oil until brown and crispy.

Serve hot with ketchup.

BESAN MEIN BREAD
(Bread in Gram Flour)

Also known as Bread Pakora, Besan Mein Bread is one of our favorite snacks! Eat it with ketchup or green chutney or just like that, tastes yummy!

We used to have this at breakfast, and when my mom made this at breakfast, she would also make "Mithi Bread" (recipe on page 166) for my grandfather. So it would be double the fun, double the taste and double the love!

Sometimes I would find this in my lunch box too and on that day, my best friend in school would be thrilled. Oh you have got "my favorite tiffin" she would say! And off we would go to our favorite place in the playground and share our lunch boxes and stories.

Those were the days!

SEVENTY THREE

Besan Mein Bread

25 MINS SERVES 2 EASY

INGREDIENTS

Gram Flour – 1 cup

Salt – as per taste

Red Chili Powder – ¼ tsp

Onions – a few pieces (finely chopped)

Bread Slices – 2 cut in half (cut in any shape; we cut in triangles)

Water – as required

Step 1: In a bowl, mix water to the gram flour slowly so that no lump are formed. The consistency of the batter should be such that it car coat the bread slices.

Step 2: Add the finely chopped onion, chili powder and salt. You can also add finely chopped coriander leaves. Add 1 tsp of oil in the batter. This keeps the snack soft.

Step 3: Now take a piece of bread and dip it in this batter such that it is coated well and deep fry in hot oil on medium to high flame til light golden brown.

Serve immediately with ketchup or chutney.

DAL CHOLA DABALA
(Lentils, Chickpeas and Bread)

Chola Dabala (Chole and bread) is a very common combination in a Sindhi household. We also make it for all of our family birthday parties.

Dal Chola Dabala is a variant of this, is a Sindhi street food and also a very famous Sindhi Song!!!! Listen to the song, "Dal Chola Dabala, Tun Khayi wan Bhal" (Lentils, Chickpeas and Bread, come and eat...)

Bread and Dal, which is a very unusual combination, is a very commonly eaten combination in any Sindhi household. I remember many a time, when Phulka would be insufficient, my mother would give us dal with bread. While there would not be other garnish like chutney or finely chopped onions or 'sev', this combination would taste just as good.

Dal sandwich is yet another street food and you will find the recipe in this book. But let's get back to Dal Chola Dabal. As the name suggests, this recipe has lentils and Chickpeas with Bread.

SEVENTY FOUR

Dal Chola Dabala

40 MINS SERVES 2 MEDIUM

INGREDIENTS

FOR DAL AND CHOLA

Moong dal – ¼ cup

Bengal Gram (Chana Dal) – ¼ cup

Chickpeas (Chola) – ¼ cup

Turmeric Powder – ¼ tsp

Coriander Powder – ½ tsp

Roasted Cumin Powder – ¼ tsp

Red Chili Powder – ¼ tsp

Mango Powder – ¼ tsp

Salt – as per taste

Oil – 1/5 tbsp (for tempering)

Cumin Seeds – ½ tsp

FOR GARNISH:

Onion – 1 finely chopped

Date-Tamarind chutney – ½ tsp

Green Chutney – ½ tsp per serving

Sev

Coriander Leaves – finely chopped

DABALA:

Preferably, use Pav (Buns). If unavailable use sliced bread.

Step 1: Soak the Moong dal and Chana dal for 3 to 4 hours. The Chola has to be soaked overnight.

Step 2: Boil the lentils and chickpeas in a pressure cooker adding water, salt and turmeric powder. I boil chickpeas separately since i takes longer.

Step 3: Once cooked, mash some of the chickpeas to give the mixture a more thick and creamy texture. Remove the lentils and chickpeas in a single vessel and mix well. Adjust salt and the consistency. The consistency should be slightly thick.

Step 4: On the lentils and chickpeas mixture, sprinkle all the spices – cumin, coriander, mango and chili powders.

Step 5: Now prepare a tempering by heating oil in a small pan When the oil is hot, add the cumin seeds and when they crackle, pou the tempering over the spices sprinkled on the lentils and chickpea mixture.

Step 6: For serving, break the pav(buns) into smaller pieces and place them on a plate. Over these pieces, pour the lentils and chickpeas mixture while it is hot.

Step 7: Next, add the chutneys, topped with finely chopped onion, then sev and finally the coriander leaves. You could also sprinkle some limejuice and sprinkle some chat masala – this is optional.

Enjoy this Sindhi Street food in the comfort of your home!

Sweet

It is surprising the many sweet dishes that we Sindhis have in our cuisine. Many are often bought from sweet shops rather than made at home but the sheer variety is admirable.

The liberal use of poppy seeds, dry fruit, milk and wheat flour is definitely something that stands out but also the different styles – Gheeyar, Satpura, Tosha which are fried varieties, Khorak or Majoon which are the typical winter specials and to top these is the Singhar ji Mithai which uses the very unique combination of milk and sev (gram flour fried noodles) – are a telling tale of the Sindhi sweet tooth!

KADHAN PRASAD
(Wheat Flour Sweet)

Kadhan Prasad is the holy offering made and served at the Gurudwara (Sikh Temple). We went to "Sukhmani" Gurudwara very often along with my mother who would do seva in the kitchen preparing for the Langar. The Prabhat Pheris and the celebration of the Guru Jayantis, bring back vivid memories of us helping at the Langar by serving the Prasad and also enjoying Langar food with family and friends.

At each of our birthdays or auspicious occasion, she would make Kadhan Prasad and first offer 'Ardaas' at the Gurudwara and then bring the blessed 'prasad' home.

When making this, do chant God's name and the Prasad will turn out aromatic and simply divine! You won't need any dry fruit and no artificial flavors. Just simply Ghee (clarified butter)/unsalted butter, wheat flour, sugar and water.

SEVENTY FIVE

Kadhan Prasad

⏱ 25 MINS   🍽 SERVES 4   👨‍🍳 EASY

INGREDIENTS

The ratio of Ghee (clarified butter)/ unsalted butter, Wheat Flour, Sugar and Water is important.

Ghee (Clarified Butter)/Unsalted Butter – 1 cup

Wheat Flour – 1 cup

Sugar – 1 cup

Water – 2 cups

Step 1: On medium flame, boil the sugar and water. Then either turn off the flame or keep at lowest.

Step 2: In a heavy bottomed pan, melt the ghee (clarified butter)/ unsalted butter and add the wheat flour. Now keep roasting the wheat flour in the ghee (clarified butter)/unsalted butter on medium to low flame till it turns light brown and starts to leave the sides of the pan.

Step 3: Roast for some more time. The color of the wheat flour should turn golden to dark brown. Turn the flame to lowest or switch it off completely. Now add the sugar water (this should be hot) and keep stirring continuously.

Take care when adding the sugar water since there will be spluttering of the roasted flour so move a little away from the pan.

Step 4: Once you have added the sugar water and the wheat flour has settled, turn the flame to lowest and continue stirring till the sugar water is absorbed completely. Then cover the pan for at least 5 minutes.

Step 5: Turn off the flame and let it rest for a few minutes before offering the Prasad.

At our home we used to (and still do), offer this Prasad along with Puris.

SINDHI LAI
(Sesame Brittle)

Sindhi Lai is a traditional sweet made during the Laal Loi festival, which is the harvest festival of the Sindhis (like Lohri, Sankranti or Pongal celebrated across India).

On this day, I remember we would also eat "Borinda" (also made from Sesame seeds but round in shape) which my grandfather would buy or which my aunt would bring from Ulhasnagar.

My mom would make triangular pieces of Lai and store them in a round steel box knowing well that these would soon be devoured! We, of course, would take pieces of it at every available opportunity until all that was left in the box were crumbs of sesame!

Make this sweet during Lal Loi or Diwali and spread the sweetness among your family and friends!

SEVENTY SIX

Sindhi Lai

⏱ 25 MINS   🍽 15 PIECES   👨‍🍳 MEDIUM

INGREDIENTS

Toasted Sesame Seeds – ¾ cup

Sugar – 1 cup

Ghee – 1 tbsp

Step 1: In a heavy bottomed pan, melt ghee and immediately add the sugar. Start caramelizing the sugar on low flame.

Step 2: When the sugar has completed melted, add the sesame seeds. The next steps are done almost immediately so keep everything ready.

Step 3: Now pour this mixture on a greased surface and using a silicon spatula, in a single direction, spread the mixture.

Step 4: Using a knife or pizza cutter lightly define the shape in which you want to break the Lai and let the mixture cool completely.

Step 5: Once the mixture cools, it will harden and easily come out of the greased surface. You can then break the brittle into smaller pieces or if you have lightly defined them in step 3, the brittle will break along those lines.

MITHI BREAD
(Sweet Bread)

Mithi Bread was my grandfather's favorite.

Coupled with Rabri or reduced sweet milk, this becomes the famous "Dabal ka Meetha". (Bread is called Dabal in Sindhi and also in many other parts in India.)

We always ate it as Mithi Bread without the sweet milk and we love it just like that. Today I make it often and in the absence of any dessert at home, this is my go-to recipe!

Enjoy this easy to make dish!

SEVENTY SEVEN

Mithi Bread

20 MINS   4 PIECES   EASY

INGREDIENTS

White Bread Slices – 2 (cut into half triangles)

Ghee/Oil – to fry

Sugar – 1 cup

Water – ½ cup

Cardamom Powder – ¼ tsp

Almond Slivers – for garnish

Step 1: In a heavy bottomed pan, on low to medium flame, deep fry the bread slices in ghee or oil until golden brown. Be careful and cautious when frying the bread since it can burn fast. You can also shallow fry the bread slices in ghee. I personally prefer the shallow fry method.

Drain on tissue paper and keep aside.

Step 2: Prepare sugar syrup by dissolving sugar in water, by bringing the water to a rolling boil. The syrup does not need to be of any specific consistency. It just needs to be thick and feel like honey or oil. Add cardamom powder.

Step 3: Now soak the fried bread in hot sugar syrup for at least 15-20 minutes before serving. This will make the bread soft. If you prefer it crunchy, soak it for about 5 minutes only.

Step 4: Garnish with almond slivers or other chopped nuts.

Serve Mithi Bread warm or cold. You could top it with a dollop of ice-cream too.

SINGHAR JI MITHAI
(Gram Flour Sweet)

Trust the Sindhis to take a traditionally savory ingredient and turn it into sweet!

Singhar is what is commonly called 'Sev'; these are fine noodles made from gram flour.

My memories of Singhar ji Mithai take me back to my childhood days when my aunt, uncle and cousins would come home over weekends with traditionally made, boxes of this sweet from Ulhasnagar! All us kids would dig our fingers right into the box and eat copious amounts of this mouth-watering delicacy dropping crumbs on the table and of course lining our mouths as we continued to play…Leaving our grandmother and aunts to clean up the sweet mess!

It has, today, become a staple in all my Diwali preparations and loved by my family and friends.

SEVENTY EIGHT

Singhar ji Mithai

⏱ 60 MINS   🍴 15 PIECES   👨‍🍳 DIFFICULT

INGREDIENTS

FOR THE UNSALTED SEV

(If unsalted sev is easily available where you live, simply use that.)

Besan (Gram Flour) – 2 cups

Oil – 1.5 tbsp

Water – to knead

Oil – to fry sev

Machine to make the sev

FOR THE MITHAI

Sev – 1½ to 2 cups

Milk – 1½ cups

Sugar – 1½ cups

Khoya (Milk Solids) – 1½ cup

Ghee (Clarified Butter) – 1.5 tbsps

Saffron – a few strands

Pistachios – for garnish

Rose Water – ¼ tsp

Silver Leaf (Varq) – for garnish

In this recipe, the sev, khoya, milk and sugar should have the same weight. I have used about 250 gms each but I have also provided the approximate measurements in cups.

SEV

Step 1: In a vessel, combine the gram flour and oil. Using water little by little make a semi-stiff dough.

Step 2: Grease the Sev Machine and put the dough in the machine.

Step 3: Heat oil over medium flame and using the sev machine, drop the sev in the hot oil. Deep fry the sev and when sev turns a light golden brown, immediately take it out and drain over a kitchen towel.

Unsalted sev is ready.

MITHAI

Step 1: In a heavy bottom pan, over medium flame, heat milk. Add sugar and cook the milk and sugar.

Step 2: Next add the Khoya in the milk. Save some (about 2 tbsps) to add later. Mix and cook; when the milk comes to a boil, add 1.5 tbsp ghee, some saffron milk and cardamom powder.

Step 3: Now lower flame, crush the sev and add it to the milk, sugar and Khoya mix. Cook for a few minutes and add rose water and remaining khoya.

Step 4: Switch off the flame, partially cover it and leave it to rest for about 30 minutes

Step 5: Grease a tray and pour this mixture. Garnish with silver leaf (Varq) and Pistachio slivers.

This sweet does not cut into pieces since it is semi-dry. Enjoy it warm; it tastes heavenly!

ATTE JA LADOON
(Wheat Flour Sweet)

Atte ja ladoon takes me back to my childhood days when we would go to my Nani's (maternal grandmother) place in Guwahati, Assam. She would make the best ladoon and this recipe is what I remember and adapted from her style.

I make atte ja ladoon many times; it is a staple at Diwali; when I am invited as guest for a party or puja, I make this sweet because they always turn out good and are a hit with everyone. They probably turn out good because it is my Nani's recipe!

My sister makes these too and she especially made them, loaded with Ghee during my post-natal phase for recovery and building back strength & stamina. Whatever the occasion, these ladoon are my favorite sweet and each time I make them, they remind me of my dearest Nani.

We all love these ladoon and I hope that this recipe will make you want to whip them up for your family and friends.

SEVENTY NINE

Atte ja Ladoon

30 MINS   12 PIECES   MEDIUM

INGREDIENTS

Wheat Flour – 2 cups

Ghee (Clarified Butter) – ½ cup

Powdered Sugar – ¾ cup

Roasted Peanuts – ¼ cup

Cardamom Powder – ½ tsp

Step 1: Heat ghee in a heavy bottom pan and roast the wheat flour on low flame until it turns aromatic and golden brown. This takes about 15 to 20 minutes.

Step 2: Switch off the flame and let this mixture cool such that it can be handled. Meanwhile, coarsely grind the roasted peanuts.

Step 3: Next add powdered sugar, cardamom powder and the ground peanuts and start making the ladoon. If the mixture is too dry and does not come together to form ladoon, heat some ghee and add to the mixture. Make the ladoon and serve or store.

This recipe traditionally uses peanuts but you can replace peanuts with almonds/cashewnuts and also add raisins. Enjoy this simple but delicious treat.

GHEEYAR
(Sweet Fritters)

Gheeyar is yet another mouth-watering delicacy and this one is associated with Holi. While Gheeyar is found in most Sindhi homes on the Holi festival, it is also a gift that traditionally, every married daughter receives from her father.

I remember that my father would send these to his sisters and to my maternal aunt (Maasi) when her parents were not in the same city.

He continued this tradition and to this day our Holi celebration is incomplete without Gheeyar. These always came from Sindhi Sweet shops in nice big colourful boxes tied with a thin ribbon, looking as good as the Gheeyar inside! Decorated with Silver Leaf (varq) and garnished with Pistachio slivers, these saffron colored, huge jalebi-like sweets are so desirable!

Today I am able to make Gheeyar at home; I think I have been able to perfect the recipe and make it my own.

EIGHTY

Gheeyar

30 MINS   10 PIECES   MEDIUM

INGREDIENTS

FOR BATTER

All Purpose Flour (Maida) - 1 cup

Yoghurt – ¼ cup

Orange Food Color – a pinch

Baking Soda – a pinch

Water as required

FOR SUGAR SYRUP

Sugar – 1 cup

Water – ½ cup

Slice of Lime

Cardamom Powder – ¼ tsp

FOR GARNISH

Pistachio Slivers

Dry Rose Petals

Silver Leaf (varq)

Step 1: Make a batter by mixing the flour, yoghurt and the food color. Add water little by little to make a thick, lump free, flowing consistency batter (The consistency of the batter must be similar to batter used for making gram flour fritters or Bhajiyas.)

Step 2: Beat air into the batter with your hands so it is light and fluffy. Cover the batter and keep aside for 8 to 10 hours or overnight.

Step 3: When you are ready to make Gheeyar, make sugar syrup by boiling sugar and water. It should be a thin syrup that feels sticky like honey.

Step 4: Add the orange food color and cardamom powder. Also add a slice of lime so that the syrup does not crystallise. Keep aside.

Step 5: Just before you are ready to fry the Gheeyar, add a pinch of baking soda to the fermented batter and mix lightly.

Step 6: In an icing cone, pour the batter and cut a small tip of the cone.

Step 7: Heat oil or ghee on medium flame. Place a metal ring in the middle of the oil (I used my 4"cake tin ring). Randomly pipe the batter within the ring.

Step 8: Allow to fry for a minute on medium flame. When the sides of the gheeyar leave the sides of the ring, take out the ring from the pan and fry the gheeyar on both sides until it is crispy.

Step 9: Dip the fried gheeyar in the sugar syrup. Sugar syrup should be luke warm. Let the gheeyar sit in the syrup for at least 30 minutes so that it can soak the sweet syrup.

Step 10: Take the gheeyar out after it has soaked in the syrup for 30 minutes, decorate the gheeyar with silver leaf (varq), pistachio slivers, dried rose petals and chopped nuts.

Enjoy this delectable sweet during Holi or any other joyful event! Serve it warm or at room temperature.

SINDHI MOHANTHAL
(Gram Flour fudge)

Mohanthal is a decadent Indian sweet very popular in the state of Rajasthan, India, but Sindhis also love this sweet and have their own unique way of making it.

My sweetest memory of Mohanthal is my brother's Thread Ceremony (Janyo in Sindhi). He must have been 8 or 10 years old and my grandfather had organized his thread ceremony with such fanfare like it was a wedding!

He had called for a cook (Radhau in Sindhi) who cooked fresh food at each meal for that day for all the guests. And during lunch there was freshly made Mohanthal! It was a beautiful occasion, elaborate ceremony and we celebrated it with our family and friends.

What stayed back were fondest memories and the lingering flavors of the food, especially Mohanthal.

Today I make the Sindhi style Mohanthal during Diwali or any other joyful event. This dark brown fudge with poppy seeds not only looks festive but tastes it too!

Sindhi Mohanthal

⏱ 60 MINS   🍽 10 PIECES   👨‍🍳 DIFFICULT

INGREDIENTS

Gram Flour (Besan) – 1 cup

Ghee – ½ cup and 1 tablespoon

Milk – 8 to 10 tbsps

Cardamom Powder – 1 tsp

Poppy Seeds – 1 tbsp

FOR SUGAR SYRUP:

Sugar – ¾ cup

Water – ½ cup

Almond Slivers – ¼ cup (for garnish)

Step 1: First, prepare the gram flour. In a vessel strain the gram flour and add 1 tablespoon of ghee and 1 tablespoons of milk. Mix with light hand and gently rub the gram flour with your hands so that the ghee and milk is mixed well.

At this time, gram flour will look like breadcrumbs. Leave it to rest for about 15 minutes.

Step 2: In a heavy bottom pan, first melt the ghee and add this Gram Flour. Roast the Gram Flour in Ghee on low flame until it becomes brown and aromatic. This takes at least 20 to 25 minutes.

Step 3: After the gram flour has turned brown and roasted well, keep adding 2 tablespoons of milk (milk should be at room temperature) each time the gram flour absorbs it. It took me about 6 tablespoons. The Sindhis make their Mohanthal darker than usual, so continue to roast to a dark brown color.

Step 4: Meanwhile prepare 'one-thread' consistency sugar syrup by boiling water and sugar.

Step 5: When sugar syrup is ready, pour the syrup into the roasted gram flour, and add poppy seeds, cardamom powder and some of the almond slivers.

Step 6: Mix well and keep stirring until all the syrup is absorbed by the gram flour and it starts to come together and leaves the bottom of the pan.

Step 7: Pour this mixture on to a greased thali (plate) and garnish with the almond slivers. Let the Mohanthal rest for 15 to 20 minutes before cutting into pieces and serving.

This Mohanthal is a semi-solid like fudge. Enjoy!

TOSHA

My memory of Tosha is of my Father's cousin bringing this box of sweet that looked like chocolate eclairs in shape, flaky and coated with very fine sugar.

It looked very different, unlike the usual ladoon, or barfi or fudge. A variation of 'Shakarpare'- a very popular Indian sweet but with its own distinct look and taste and now a very common addition to my Diwali fare.

EIGHTY TWO

Tosha

45 MINS   8 PIECES   DIFFICULT

INGREDIENTS

Maida/All Purpose Flour – 3/4 cup

Ghee – 2 tsp

Sugar – 2 tbsps

Water – ¼ cup

Oil – to deep fry

FOR SUGAR SYRUP

Water – ¼ cup

Sugar – ½ cup

Step 1: Dissolve the sugar in water by simply mixing the two. You don't need to boil the water or make a sugar syrup for kneading the dough.

Step 2: In a vessel combine the flour and ghee. Mix well; the flour should look like breadcrumbs and when you hold the flour in your palm and press with your fingers, it should hold shape. This means there's enough ghee and you don't need to add any more.

Step 3: Now using the sugar water prepared in step 1, knead a stiff dough and let it rest for 10 – 15 minutes.

Step 4: Divide the dough into equal portions and roll the portions with your palms into cylindrical shaped Toshas about 2 inches long.

Step 5: Heat oil in heavy bottom pan and put one Tosha in the oil. If it does not break, add all of the Tosha and reduce the flame to low. (If it breaks when you check one, it means that it has too much ghee and just add more flour and knead the dough again).

Step 6: Keep moving the Tosha in the oil so that they are evenly golden colored. Then remove and drain on kitchen towel.

Step 7: Now in a pan prepare sugar syrup. Boil the water and sugar and make a thick syrup. The syrup needs to be thick and feel like oil or honey.

Step 8: Add the Toshas in this syrup and let the Toshas absorb all of the syrup. When all of the syrup is absorbed, switch off the flame and let Tosha stay in the pan until all of the moisture dries up.

Step 9: Take them out and let them rest for at least an hour until they have cooled down to room temperature and then serve.

Serve Tosha at room temperature as snack or dessert.

ATTE JA MALPURA
(Wheat Flour sweet pancakes)

This Malpura dish is special in that it is not dunked in sugar syrup. In fact it is moist and mildly sweet; can be served just like that minus the usual Semolina Fudge or Suji jo Seero.

At home, Malpura's got made rarely and only on very special occasions or on those lazy Sunday afternoons for an early brunch.

Nowadays I make Malpura when I have guests or on any other festive occasion or celebration. Traditionally this recipe is made with wheat flour only; but there are a number of variations that use semolina and all purpose flour too.

EIGHTY THREE

Atte ja Malpura

🕐 40 MINS   🍽 15 PIECES   👨‍🍳 MEDIUM

INGREDIENTS

Wheat Flour – 1 cup

Sugar – ½ cup

Cardamom Powder – ¼ tsp

Black Peppercorns – 5 to 6

Water – 1 cup (The amount of water depends on the flour. This is how much I needed)

Ghee/Oil – to fry

Step 1: Make a batter by combining wheat flour, sugar and water. Add water little by little so that its lump free, thick and of flowing consistency.

Step 2: Leave it to rest for at least 15 to 20 minutes. The consistency of the batter should be similar to the batter used for making gram flour fritters or Bhajiyas.

Step 3: In a heavy bottomed pan, heat some ghee/oil on medium flame to fry the Malpuras. Lower the flame and pour a ladle of the batter such that it forms a disc shape of not more than 3 to 4" in diameter.

Step 4: On medium flame fry the Malpura until it is golden brown on both sides. Follow this process for the rest of the batter.

Serve Malpuro warm. If you want the dish richer, serve it with seero or rabdi.

KHEERNI
(Sweetened Milk with Sago)

Kheerni is a delightful sweet dish made with very simple ingredients – milk, sugar and Sago (Sabudana), but one that tastes decadent and rich.

At home, my mother used to make Kheerni on any auspicious day or when she had to prepare 'Bhog' (Offering to God).

We love Kheerni just as dessert and I include it in my Diwali dinner these days.

EIGHTY FOUR

Kheerni

45 MINS   SERVES 4   MEDIUM

INGREDIENTS

Sago (Sabudana) – ¼ cup

Whole Milk – 2 ¼ cups

Cardamom Powder – ½ tsp

Sugar – ½ cup

Dry Fruit – ¼ cup (Cashewnuts, Almond, Pistachio Slivers and Raisins)

Ghee – 2 tbsp

Water – to soak Sago

Saffron Strands – Optional

Step 1: Wash the sago a few times and then soak in water. To soak, I use the same amount of water as sago. Soak for 3 to 4 hours.

Step 2: Take a heavy bottom pan on which you will make the Kheerni and first grease it with ghee. This will ensure that the sago pearls don't stick to the pan.

Step 3: When the pan is slightly hot, add the soaked sago and lightly roast them for 2 to 3 minutes so that some of the moisture dries up. Then add the milk and saffron strands if using. Stir continuously and let the milk come to a boil on medium flame.

Step 4: Add sugar and mix well. You can adjust the amount of sugar based on preference. I first add a little less than ½ cup and adjust if I need more.

Step 5: When the sago pearls become translucent and rise up, it means they are completely cooked. At this time, add the cardamom powder and let the Kheerni simmer on low flame. Keep stirring at regular intervals.

Step 6: In the meanwhile in a smaller pan on low flame, heat ghee and lightly roast the almond slivers and cashewnuts. When they turn lightly brown, add pistachio slivers and raisins. Roast only for a few seconds after adding raisins and then add these ghee roasted dry fruit to the Kheerni.

Step 7: Stir for some time and then switch off the flame. The consistency of the Kheerni should be slightly thick.

Garnish with dried rose petals if you have and enjoy this simple dessert! I like it warm.

PUJA JI KUTTI
(Pounded Wheat Bread Sweet)

This recipe is the fried version of the Kutti recipe mentioned earlier. This one takes longer to make, tastes great and is served as Prasad or holy offering during a Puja.

My mother made it for Ganeshchauth and Satyanarayan Pujas and boy how I wished that she would make it everyday! It tasted so good; I remember I would wipe clean the container using my fingers to make all the leftover pieces stick to them so I could lick off the Kutti.

While I make this Kutti occasionally, I make a good amount that can last us for a couple of weeks. We control ourselves by just taking a spoon or two to fulfill the desires of our sweet tooth (nay teeth!)

EIGHTY FIVE

Puja ji Kutti

⏱ 30 MINS   🍽 SERVES 4   👨‍🍳 MEDIUM

INGREDIENTS

Wheat Flour – 1 cup

Oil/Ghee – 2 tbsp (more depending on how it comes together as explained in the steps)

Water – to knead the dough

Oil – to deep fry

Sugar – ½ cup

Step 1: In a vessel place the wheat flour and add the oil/ghee with light fingers incorporating it well in the flour. Once you have mixed the oil/ghee into the flour when you hold it in your hand and press it, it should hold the shape and not crumble. This means that the flour has sufficient fat.

Now add water little by little and make a semi stiff dough.

Step 2: Heat oil in a frying pan. In the meanwhile, roll the dough with a rolling pin and make a disc shaped bread about ½ inch in thickness. Now using a pizza cutter or knife cut this into medium sized triangles.

Step 3: On medium to low flame, fry these triangles until they are crisp and golden brown. Ensure that the flame is medium to low so that they are cooked all through and stay crisp. Next, remove them from the pan and drain on a kitchen towel.

Step 4: Let these fried wheat triangles cool completely. Next put them in a blender and blend them into smaller pieces. (My mother would break these pieces in the mortar pestle since we did not have a blender in those days.) So when using a blender pulse the pieces for just 2 or 3 times so that you don't make it a powder.

Step 5: Take the ground pieces out in a container, add the sugar, and mix well. Adjust the sugar based on the degree of sweetness you like and serve.

Optionally, you could add cardamom powder, almond slivers and even broken cashew nuts.

Serve at room temperature as breakfast, snack or even dessert.

PETHE JO SEERO
(Pumpkin fudge)

Pumpkin is such a versatile fruit. Both, sweet and savory dishes made in the Indian kitchens using Pumpkin taste so appetizing.

But I think we Sindhis are a little partial to its use in our sweets. We love Pethe jo Seero just as we do Gajjar jo seero (Carrot Fudge) and Kadu-a-jo seero (Bottle gourd fudge).

The lovely saffron color, the poppy seeds, the dry fruit garnish all make Pethe jo Seero so desirable. As kids I think this was my mother's way to feed us this very healthy and nourishing fruit and what better way than to make a dessert for us three kids all of who had quite a sweet tooth (though I think my elder sister beat us hands down!!!)

I make Pethe Jo Seero many a times, especially in the winters; the freshly made seero bringing us warmth and cheer!

EIGHTY SIX

Pethe jo Seero

45 MINS SERVES 4 MEDIUM

INGREDIENTS

Petho (Pumpkin) – 1½ cups (grated)

Ghee – 2 tbsps

Milk – 1½ cups

Sugar – ½ cup

Poppy Seeds – 1 tbsp

Cardamom Powder – ½ tsp

Dry Fruit – ¼ cup (Almond and Pistachio slivers and Raisins)

Step 1: In a heavy bottomed pan, heat the ghee. Add the grated pumpkin, and saute on low flame until the pumpkin is soft.

Step 2: Add the milk, cardamom powder, raisins and poppy seeds and cook until the milk is almost absorbed completely.

Step 3: Add the sugar. You can add more and adjust for sweetness based on your preference. Cook the mixture until sugar dissolves and the mixture begins to leave the sides of the pan.

Serve warm garnished with almond and pistachio slivers.

CHOORI

Choori is wheat flour based Prasad or holy offering made especially during Satyanarayana Puja. I remember eating Choori from a piece of newspaper used to serve the Prasad at the temple. My mother would also make it during Pujas and almost always on Satyanarayana Puja. And all of us would love this Prasad or holy offering so much, we could have it as a meal! But of course we were not allowed because of all the sugar that it has!

The key to getting Choori right is roasting the wheat flour enough that it does not stick in your mouth or throat while eating. Make it during your Puja and other holy occasions or make it just like that as desert!

EIGHTY SEVEN

Choori

⏱ 15 MINS   🍽 SERVES 3   👨‍🍳 EASY

INGREDIENTS

Wheat Flour – 1.5 cups

Sugar – 1 cup

Ghee – ¼ cup

Cardamom Powder – ¼ tsp

Almond Slivers – ¼ cup

Step 1: Melt the ghee in a heavy bottom pan, add the wheat flour. On low heat, roast the wheat flour till it turns a nice golden brown and aromatic.

Step 2: Take the pan off the flame and when the mixture has cooled, add the sugar, cardamom powder and almond slivers.

Serve Choori at room temperature along with some fruit.

PRAGHREE/PRAGREE
(Sindhi Gujiya)

Holi is a very special event for the Sindhis. Along with the colors, the pre-holi event – burning the Holika and preparing 'Roat' is also unique. More about that later, but for now here's the recipe for Praghree.

Like Gheeyar, this sweet is also prepared during Holi and sent to a married daughters' home on the day. Stuffed with sweet Mawa/Khoya, dry fruit and dipped in sugar syrup, it is decadent, delicious and rich all at the same time!

While making Praghree calls for a lot of patience and work, the result is all worth it.

EIGHTY EIGHT

Praghree

🕐 75 MINS   🍽 4 PIECES   👨‍🍳 DIFFICULT

INGREDIENTS

FOR THE STUFFING:

Unsweetened Khoya – ½ cup

Sugar – ½ cup

Cardamom Powder – ½ tsp

Assorted Dry Fruit (Cashewnuts, Almonds, Pistachios) – ¼ cup

FOR THE SUGAR SYRUP:

Sugar – ½ cup

Water – little more than ¼ cup

Cardamom Powder – ¼ tsp

Lemon Juice – ½ tsp

Saffron Strands (optional)

FOR THE DOUGH:

All Purpose Flour (Maida) – 1 cup

Ghee – 1 ½ tbsp

Water as required to knead the dough

FOR THE PASTE:

Ghee – 1 ½ tbsp.

All Purpose Flour (Maida) – 1 tbsp

STUFFING

Step 1: To make the stuffing, shred the Mawa/Khoya and in a heavy bottom pan, roast it on low heat until it becomes completely dry. Keep aside to cool.

Step 2: Meanwhile, grind the sugar. Chop the dry fruit and roast them on low flame in just a spoonful of ghee for about 2 to 3 minutes.

When the Mawa/Khoya cools, crumble it and add the sugar, dry fruit & cardamom powder. The stuffing is ready. Keep it aside.

DOUGH

Step 1: To make dough, in a vessel combine the flour and only some of the ghee and incorporate it in the flour such that it resembles breadcrumbs.

To check if there is enough ghee in the flour, hold some in your hand and press with your fingers. If it holds shape, it means there is enough and you should not add any more.

Step 2: Adding water slowly, (not all at once); knead into a semi soft dough. Cover with a damp cloth and keep aside.

SUGAR SYRUP

Step 1: Prepare sugar syrup by boiling water and sugar. Add cardamom powder and saffron strands (optional). The sugar syrup must be thick but not of any specific 'thread consistency'.

Add some lemon juice to prevent the syrup from crystalizing.

ROLLING THE PRAGHREE

Step 1: Divide the dough into 2 or 3 equal portions. Take one of the portions (keep the other portion covered with the damp cloth) and roll it into a big disc of about 7 or 8" in diameter.

Step 2: Using the mouth of a small glass (3" diameter), or any othe cookie cutter, make smaller discs from this big disc. (I got four smalle discs in this way).

Step 3: Now apply the paste on the top of each disc and stack the 4 discs, one on top of the other (do not apply paste on the top of the fourth disc)

Step 4: With the rolling pin, but with a light hand, roll the stacked up disc: some more such that you get one layered disc of about 5" in diameter.

Step 5: Take a small spoon of the stuffing, place it in the center of this disc, and apply water around the stuffing (not on the edges).

Step 6: Fold the disc and lightly press around the stuffing so that it is sealed and does not come out when frying the praghree.

Roll the other Praghrees in the same way.

FRYING THE PRAGHREE

Step 1: Heat oil in a heavy bottom pan. On low flame, deep-fry each Praghree until it is golden brown on both sides and you can clearly see the layers of the discs.

Step 2: Ensure that the sugar syrup is warm (not hot). As soon as you take out the Praghree from the oil, dip it in the sugar syrup.

Step 3: Let each Praghree stay in the sugar syrup for about 5 minutes. This will allow the sugar syrup to seep through all of the layers.

Step 4: After the Praghrees have soaked in the sugar syrup, plate the praghrees and garnish with silver leaf, pistachio slivers and edible dry rose petals.

Serve during your Holi celebration or any other joyful event and enjoy with your family and friends!

MAJOON
(Royal Dry Fruit and milk Sweet)

Majoon is very similar to a dry fruit barfi (sweet). Made with milk, dry fruit, ghee and sugar, and all things decadent! In many families, this is also made with Urad Dal but this special 'barfi' recipe uses milk and milk solids (khoya).

Majoon is also a special winter treat. In the past, this sweet used to be made in bulk to be sent to the houses of married daughters and to be consumed in the house. Very nutritious - because it has the goodness of dry fruit and milk - I too make this, but in small quantities and usually at Diwali.

Enjoy Majoon – this royal Sindhi sweet!

EIGHTY NINE

Majoon

⏱ 70 MINS 🍽 15 PIECES 👨‍🍳 DIFFICUL

INGREDIENTS

Milk – 3 ½ cups (Whole Milk)

Sugar – 1 ¼ cups

Poppy Seeds – 6 tbsps

Cardamom Powder – 2 tsps

Dried Dates – ¼ cup

Dry Fruit – 1 ½ cups

Milk Solids (Khoya) – 1 ½ cups

Desiccated Coconut – ½ cup

Ghee – 6 to 8 tbsps

Silver Leaf (Varq) – optional for decoration

Step 1: In a heavy bottom pan, on medium flame heat the milk stirring continuously. When the milk is hot enough, add the sugar and let the milk come to a boil.

Step 2: On low flame, add the poppy seeds and cardamom powde and keep stirring continuously to ensure that milk does not stick to the bottom of the pan. By now, the milk should have reduced and the mixture would have become thicker. Add the dried dates too.

Step 3: In a separate pan, on low flame, heat 4 tbsps of ghee and roast the milk solids (Khoya) until it turns a very light golden brown Add the desiccated coconut and roast with the khoya until it turns aromatic. We do not have to change the color of the coconut.

Step 4: Now add the roasted Khoya and desiccated coconut into the milk mixture all the while stirring on low flame. Add the dry fruit now (save some for garnish) and mix well; add the remaining 2 tbsps of ghee now. Keep stirring until the mixture comes together. If you think the mixture needs some more ghee, add the last 2 tbsps. (I did not have to use these)

Step 5: Keep stirring on low flame, until everything comes together and the mixture begins to leave the sides of the pan. The moisture should have completely dried up and your Majoon is now ready.

Step 6: At this time pour the Majoon on a greased thali (plate). If available, decorate with silver leaf (varq) and garnish with some almond and pistachio slivers.

Step 7: Let the mixture set for at least 7 to 8 hours before cutting into pieces. After you have cut it in pieces in the thali (plate), leave it in the refrigerator to set for at least 3 to 4 hours before taking out the pieces for storage.

Serve this as dessert especially during the winters.

KUTTI
(Pounded Wheat Bread sweet)

Kutti is an unimaginable sweet food eaten mostly at breakfast and made from left over 'phulka'/rotis! I think we call it Kutti because 'kut' in Sindhi means 'to pound/grind'. And Kutti is also made by grinding the left over phulka/rotis.

My childhood memories of Kutti are naturally 'sweet'. With a lot of homemade ghee, sugar and love, this simple but endearing dish always left us wanting for more!

My mother used to serve Kutti in steel katoris (small bowls) and we would eat with our fingers licking away the sugar and ghee, happily talking about school and other fun stories from class!

NINETY

Kutti

⏱ 10 MINS   🍴 SERVES 2   👨‍🍳 EASY

INGREDIENTS

Phulka/Rotis – 2

Ghee – 2 tbsp (add more if you like it decadent)

Sugar – 1 tbsp (add more if you like it sweeter)

Step 1: Fold each phulko/roti into a triangle; using a rolling pin break the phulka/rotis into smaller pieces.

Step 2: In a heavy bottomed pan, heat some ghee, add these pieces of phulka/rotis, give it a stir and switch off the flame.

Step 3: Sprinkle the sugar on top and Kutti is ready to serve.

Sometimes I add some cardamom powder and if I am feeling festive, some almond slivers too! Serve Kutti warm.

KHUS KHUS JO SEERO
(Poppy Seeds Fudge)

Khus Khus jo Seero is a very rich dessert. Made with poppy seeds and full of dry fruit, this dessert is both decadent and healthy – of course when eaten in small quantities!

In many homes, this dessert is made during Raksha Bandhan (Indian festival for brothers and sisters) and often without sugar because poppy seeds and the dried dates in this recipe lend it a sweet taste.

I, however, make this seero with sugar and love it when it is slightly warm, the khus khus melting in my mouth!

NINETY ONE

Khus Khus jo Seero

40 MINS   SERVES 2   MEDIUM

INGREDIENTS

Poppy Seeds – ½ cup

Ghee – 3 tbsps

Milk – 1½ cups

Sugar – ½ cup

Cardamom Powder – ½ tsp

Saffron Strands – 8 to 10 (optional)

Dried Dates – ¼ cup (pitted and chopped into small pieces)

Dry fruit (Almond and Pistachio Slivers , Raisins, Cashewnuts, Melon Seeds, Chironji/Charoli Nuts) – 1 cup

Silver Leaf (Varq) – for garnish

Step 1: Soak the poppy seeds in water for a few hours or overnight. The following morning, blend the seeds into a very smooth paste. When you feel the paste between your index finger and thumb it should feel completely smooth.

Step 2: In a heavy bottom pan, on medium flame, heat the ghee and add the poppy seed paste. Keep stirring the paste on low flame until the poppy seeds turn light brown taking care that the paste does not stick to the pan. Roasting the poppy seed paste in the ghee is the most important step in this dessert.

Step 3: When the paste is roasted to a nice brown color, add the milk (which should be at room temperature) and now stir on medium flame. When the milk comes to a boil, lower the flame and add the sugar, cardamom powder, saffron strands if using, the dried dates and dry fruit (save some almond and pistachio slivers for garnish).

Step 4: Keep stirring on medium to low flame until the milk is completely absorbed by the paste and the mixture begins to release ghee and leave the sides of the pan.

Step 5: Switch off the flame, take the seero out in a serving bowl and decorate with silver varq and the almond and pistachio slivers.

Serve this decadent dessert warm in the winters.

MITHA SATPURA
(Sweet Seven Big Rotis)

Crispy and sweet, Satpura looks and tastes delicious. It is literally made of 7 ('Sat' in Sindhi) Puras (Rotis) and is a wheel of taste, crunch and size!

Found mostly in sweet shops, this Sindhi delight is made especially during Mahalaxmi Puja (Mahalakshmi-a-jo-Sagro). When I make them at home, I make them of a smaller size so that they are easier to handle.

Try this super delicious sweet and make them for your family and friends.

197

NINETY TWO

Mitha Satpura

45 MINS   6 PIECES   DIFFICUL

INGREDIENTS

FOR THE DOUGH

All Purpose Flour/Maida – 1 cup

Salt – a pinch

Water – as required

FOR THE PASTE

Ghee – 3 tbsps

All Purpose Flour/Maida– 2 tbsp

FOR GARNISH

Powdered Sugar – ¼ cup

Cardamom Powder – ½ tsp

Pistachio Slivers – for garnish

FOR FRYING

Oil

Step 1: In a vessel, combine the flour and salt. Using water, make a soft Phulka like dough. Cover and let the dough rest for about 15 minutes.

Step 2: In a small bowl add 2 tbsps of flour to 3 tbsps ghee to make a paste. The paste should have a flowing consistency so you can easil apply it when you roll the dough.

Step 3: Make 7 small portions of the dough and with a rolling pin, rol each portion into a very thin disc shaped bread of about 8" diameter When rolling, sprinkle enough flour to roll these into 7 thin discs.

Step 4: Apply the ghee and flour paste on the first disc and then sprinkle some flour. Then stack the next on top of it and so on. Before stacking each disc, remember to apply and spread the ghee and flou paste and sprinkle the flour.

Step 5: After you have stacked all the discs – one on top of the other apply the ghee and flour paste on the top most disc as well.

Step 6: Cut these stacked discs into strips. Take each strip, roll it or your index finger, tuck the edge of the strip into the center and keep aside. Press it down gently.

Step 7: Now with a nicely greased rolling pin, roll this into a bigge disc of about 5" in diameter taking care that you roll it gently. Rol each Satpura just before you are ready to fry it.

Step 8: Fry the Satpura on medium flame. While frying, try to separate the layers using a long spoon or knife, so that all the layers are seen.

These should be a very light brown color and not too brown.

Step 9: When the Satpura is fried, drain it on a kitchen towel. Sprinkle with powdered sugar and cardamom powder and garnish with Pistachio slivers.

Serve at room temperature as dessert or snack.

KADU-A-JO SEERO
(Bottle Gourd sweet fudge)

Kadu-a-jo Seero is a mildly sweet dessert and a fine way to camouflage the bottle gourd! The beautiful, pastel green color of the seero with poppy seeds and ghee roasted cashews makes it soothing to look at and appetizing too.

As kids I think we were partial to the red gajrun jo seero (Carrot fudge), but nowadays I like Kadu-a-jo seero equally.

Serve it as dessert to your friends and family!

NINETY THREE

Kadu-a-jo Seero

25 MINS　　SERVES 2　　EASY

INGREDIENTS

Bottle Gourd – 1 cup (grated)

Milk – 3 cups

Ghee – 3 tbsps

Sugar – ¼ cup

Cardamom Powder – ½ tsp

Poppy Seeds – 1 tbsp

Dry Fruit (Pistachio and Almond Slivers, Cashew Nuts and Raisins) – ½ cup

Step 1: In a heavy bottom pan, heat 2 ½ tbsps of ghee on low flame and sauté the grated bottle gourd for about 5 minutes. Next add the milk, poppy seeds, raisins and cardamom powder. Keep stirring until the milk reduces.

Step 2: Add the sugar and keep stirring. Meanwhile, in a separate small pan, heat ½ tbsp ghee and roast some cashewnuts and almond slivers. Once these are well roasted, add them to the bottle gourd and milk mixture.

Step 3: One all the moisture has reduced and the seero comes together and leaves the sides of the pan, it is ready. Plate and garnish with pistachio and almond slivers and serve.

Serve warm as dessert or even as breakfast.

KHORAK
(Wheat Flour Sweet)

Khorak is a very rich winter sweet. Made with wheat flour, ghee and loaded with dry fruit, it is said to be ideal for new mothers to gain the much needed post-partum strength. While I am not sure of that, I am sure of its drool-worthy taste and the fact that you cannot stop, at eating just one piece.

You will see the use of poppy seeds in this sweet too and I think we Sindhis use poppy seeds generously in all our desserts except the fried ones perhaps (like Tosha or Satpura).

Khorak is an easy to make sweet; roasting of the wheat flour to perfection is its hallmark. Once that is done, Khorak turns out wonderfully well and it will also finish in no time!

NINETY FOUR

Khorak

🕐 **60 MINS**   🍴 **30 PIECES**   👨‍🍳 **DIFFICUL**

INGREDIENTS

Wheat Flour – 2 cups

Ghee – ¼ cup for frying the edible gum and 1 cup for roasting the flour

Poppy Seeds – ¼ cup

Melon Seeds – ¼ cup

Water – 1 cup

Sugar – 2 cups

Dry Fruit – 1 cup

Dried Dates – ½ cup

Desiccated Coconut- ¼ cup

Edible Gum – 3 tbsps

Cardamom Powder – 1 tbsp

Note: In this recipe, if you are using measurements in grams, use equal weight of wheat flour, sugar and Ghee (250 grams), 50 gms of edible gum and 125 ml water. The rest of the ingredients (dry fruit, melon seeds, desiccated coconut, dried dates and poppy seeds), you could alter based on availability and preference.

Step 1: In a vessel, dissolve the sugar in the water. You don't need to boil the water or make any syrup. Let the sugar dissolve while you complete the rest of the steps for the Khorak.

Step 2: Chop all dry fruit into small pieces. Pit the dried dates and cut them. Dry roast the melon seeds and the poppy seeds separately. Prepare a greased thali (plate) and sprinkle with poppy seeds, almond slivers and some desiccated coconut.

Step 3: In a heavy bottom pan, heat the ghee and when it is hot, fry the edible gum. Take it out and drain once the pieces swell like small popcorn. Let the gum cool completed before blending it into powder.

Step 4: In the same pan, add some more ghee and the wheat flour. On low flame, roast the wheat flour until it turns aromatic and turns golden brown. This takes at least about 20 minutes.

Step 5: Next, add the poppy seeds, mix well and keep stirring while roasting it along with the wheat flour for at least 4 to 5 minutes.

Step 6: Next add the crushed edible gum and mix well for 2 minutes. At this time mix in the cardamom powder and the desiccated coconut.

Step 7: Add all of the dry fruit, melon seeds and dried dates. Mix well. Now add the sugar water. When you add the sugar water, ensure that the flame is at its lowest.

Step 8: When the sugar water is mixed well, increase the flame to medium and mix everything well till the sugar water is absorbed completely, the mixture begins to harden, leave the sides of the pan and release ghee. All these are signs that the Khorak is ready.

Step 9: Take it out onto the greased thali, garnish with almond and pistachio slivers. Let it set for at least 3 to 4 hours before cutting it to pieces.

Serve at room temperature as dessert especially in the winters.

BORINDA
(Sesame Seed Sweet Balls)

Laal Loi is the Sindhi festival of harvest and is celebrated on the 13th of Jan every year by lighting a bonfire and going around it, offering Ber (Jujuba fruit), red carrots and Sesame seeds.

We used to get Borinda (sesame seeds balls) and Rewdi (Sesame Seeds candy) on this day. I remember that my grandfather would get the Borinda on his way back from work or my aunt would get them from Ulhasnagar. These would be big and very hard to eat and often we would use the pestle (mortar pestle) to break them into smaller, manageable pieces that could fit in our little mouths!

Unlike the very common Tilgud, these sesame sweets don't use jaggery, instead they use sugar. These are very traditional and they look as nice as they taste!

NINETY FIVE

Borinda

30 MINS   8 PIECES   MEDIUM

INGREDIENTS

Sesame Seeds – 1 cup

Sugar – 1 cup

Water – 1½ tbsps

Lemon Juice – ½ tbsp

Ghee – 1 tsp

Step 1: In a heavy bottom pan, first dry roast the sesame seeds, on low flame for two minutes, take them out in a bowl and keep aside.

Step 2: In the same pan, on lowest flame, heat 1½ tbsps of water, add the lemon juice and then add the sugar. Keep stirring on low flame.

Step 3: Continue stirring the sugar continuously on low flame. To check if the sugar syrup is ready, in a bowl of water, drop a little of the syrup. (If it settles below without spreading, it is ready. When you take it out of the water, it is hard and when you drop it in the bowl, it sounds like glass.)

Step 4: Once the syrup is ready, all the next steps have to be completed immediately. Mix in the sesame seeds well and switch off the flame.

Step 5: Next with a spoon, scoop out some of the sesame seed and sugar syrup mix, wet your palms with water and make a ball. Since the mixture is hot, use the spoon and water to make the balls.

Make all the balls in this way and while the mixture is warm/hot since once the sugar syrup cools, it becomes hard and then it may not be possible to give it the desired shape.

Serve these to your family and friends after they have completely cooled.

JUAR JI KUTTI
(Pounded bread made of sorghum flour)

There are so many different ways of making Kutti and while we usually make this with Wheat Flour, here is one that we also make with Juar jo atto (Sorghum Flour).

The recipe is very similar to the fried version of the wheat flour kutti (recipe on page 193).

NINETY SIX

Juar ji Kutti

30 MINS   **SERVES 2**   **MEDIUM**

INGREDIENTS

Sorghum Flour – ½ cup

Ghee – 1 tsp

Cardamom Powder – ¼ tsp

Water as required

Oil – to deep fry

Sugar – ½ cup

Water – ¾ cup

Step 1: In a vessel, combine the sorghum flour and ghee. Mix the ghee well into the flour with your fingers such that the flour resemble breadcrumbs. Then hold some of the flour in your palm and pres with your fingers. If the flour holds shape, then there is enough ghee in the flour and you do not need to add any more.

Step 2: Using water, knead a semi-soft dough. Make small oblong shaped portions and deep-fry them in oil on low flame. Always fr these on low flame so that they are well fried, both inside and outside

Step 3: When these portions turn a light brown, remove them from the oil and drain them on a kitchen towel.

Step 4: Meanwhile make sugar syrup by boiling water and sugar. Add cardamom powder. The sugar syrup should feel thick like honey and should not be of any specific 'thread consistency'. Keep aside.

Step 5: When the fried portions have cooled, break them into pieces and blend them into smaller pieces resembling breadcrumbs. Take them out in a bowl.

Step 6: Pour the hot sugar syrup on the juar crumbs and mix well with a spoon so that the syrup is mixed well with the crumbs. Kutti should still look like moist crumbs so pour only so much syrup.

Garnish with almond slivers and serve.

Serve warm or at room temperature at your breakfast table.

BHUGAL MAWO/ BHUGAL MAWA
(Sautéed and Sweetened Reduced Milk)

What a decadent sweet this one and how delicious! Yet another sweet that takes a long time to make, but makes all the wait worthwhile!

Easy to make, uses only 3 ingredients and it never ceases to amaze me how such dishes were conceptualized!

We used to get this sweet rarely and in very small quantities! My mom would make it on those rare occasions when the milk curdled on its own (because of weather etc). Instead of using it as Paneer in a vegetable dish, she would make this sweet. And the three of us would wonder why it was never enough and we would be craving for some more to satisfy our sweet tooth!

I make Bhugal Mawa whenever I make Pragree and during the many festive occasions, we celebrate.

NINETY SEVEN

Bhugal Mawo

🕐 60 MINS   🍽 SERVES 4   👨‍🍳 MEDIUM

INGREDIENTS

Milk – 2 litres or 8 cups

Cardamom Powder – ½ tsp

Lemon Juice – ¼ tsp
OR
Edible Alum (powdered) – a pinch

Sugar – 1 cup

Ghee – 4 tbsps

Almond Slivers – ¼ cup for garnish

Silver Leaf (Varq) – for garnish

Step 1: In a heavy bottomed pan, on high flame, bring the milk to a boil. Remember to stir continuously. Since the flame is high, you have to be cautious that the milk does not overflow when it reaches the boiling point.

Step 2: After the first boil, lower the flame to low, add cardamom powder and stir continuously until the milk reduces by half. This takes at least 30 odd minutes depending on the quantity of milk.

Step 3: Once the milk has reduced to half, add the lemon juice or the alum. Remember that this amount has to be very little. If it is even slightly more, the mawa will become chewy. (Note – I have tried both lemon juice and alum and I believe the result from the lemon juice is slightly better.)

Step 4: Once you have added the juice, stop stirring for about 2 minutes to allow the milk to start the curdling process. After this time, you need to start stirring again and you will see that the milk has started to curdle and get grainy.

Step 5: From this point, you need to be stirring continuously. (If you don't, the milk may stick to the bottom and burn). Now add the sugar in small quantities (not all at once) and stir continuously until sugar dissolves. When the mixture begins to thicken add 2 tablespoons of ghee and continue stirring. After some time, add the rest of the ghee.

Step 6: Keep stirring until the mawa turns a light brown and starts to leave the sides of the pan. These are signs that the mawa is done. At this time take it out in a bowl and garnish with almond slivers and varq. If you leave it to rest, it will harden very slightly and you will be able to cut it into pieces too.

Serve warm or at room temperature as your mouthwatering dessert. I like to serve this warm.

THAADAL
(Cool nut-based sweet milk)

Thaadal is a very cool and refreshing drink and probably comes from the word Thado (meaning cold in Sindhi). It is made from almonds, melon, poppy seeds and a number of other ingredients.

We didn't make Thaadal at home but we would always get it during the Mahashivratri Puja and the Holi Puja at the temple inside the Sindhi Society, very close to where I lived. The three of us would have our share of this healthy drink at the temple and we would also carry an empty steel kettle so we could take some back for the household!

This is a constant at all Holi parties and while I make it at home today, I still miss enjoying this wholesome drink at the temple with family and friends!

NINETY EIGHT

Thaadal

10 MINS   SERVES 4   EASY

INGREDIENTS

Almonds – 1 cup

Melon Seeds (Charmagaz) – 2 tbsp

Poppy Seeds – ½ tsp

Fennel Seeds – ½ tbsp

Cardamom Powder – ½ tsp

Black Pepper (whole) – 8 to 10

Dried Rose Petals (if available) – 15 to 20

Whole Milk – 3 cups

Sugar – 1 cup

Step 1: Soak all the ingredients (except milk and sugar) in about 3 cups of water for at least 3 – 4 hours or overnight.

Step 2: Grind all of these ingredients into a paste using some of the water in which the ingredients were soaked. Next using a muslin cloth or a nut milk bag, strain all the milk from this paste.

After the milk has been strained, grind the ingredients again to get the rest of the juice from the ingredients.

Step 3: To this nut milk, now add the chilled whole milk. You could add all of the 3 cups or based on the concentration of the nut milk increase, or decrease the amount.

Step 4: Add the sugar. Here you can increase or decrease the amount based on your taste. Once it dissolves, Thaadal is ready to serve.

Serve it chilled, garnished with rose petals and a few strands of saffron.

CHOTHE/MITHI TIKKI/ MAHALAKSHMI ROT
(Fried Wheat Flour Sweet Bread)

I serve these to my son as cookies! Or at least I tell him, these are 'like cookies' and he enjoys them…at least sort of! These yummy triangular or round or diamond shaped pieces are a bite of divine! Literally and metaphorically speaking because these are served as Prasad or holy offering during 'Mahalakshmi' (Indian Goddess of wealth and prosperity) Puja (holy event) in a Sindhi household.

While this goes by so many different names, as kids we simply called it 'Cut Cut'!!! My mother would make this for us - after making necessary portions for the puja and prasad- in the shape of diamonds. She would do this by first rolling the dough into a big round disc and then using the knife, cut the disc into many small diamonds! We in our childish banter called it 'cut cut' and so the name stuck! And in our house it still goes by that name!

Make this for your Mahalakshmi Puja or for your family and friends whenever you feel like eating a crispy taste of sweetness!

NINETY NINE

Mithi Tikki

🕐 30 MINS   🍽 12 PIECES   👨‍🍳 MEDIUM

INGREDIENTS

Wheat Flour – 1 cup

OR

Wheat – ½ cup

All Purpose Flour – ½ cup

OR

All Purpose Flour – 1 cup

Water – ½ cup

Sugar – 5 tbsp

Ghee – 3 to 4 tsp

Cardamom Powder – ½ tsp

Oil – for deep frying

Step 1: Dissolve the sugar in the water by leaving it for a couple of hours. You can also dissolve the sugar in water by boiling the water and sugar (you do not have to worry about syrup consistency; the sugar simply needs to dissolve in the water) but always cool the water to room temperature before using.

Step 2: In a vessel, combine the flours if using both wheat and all purpose flour. I have used only wheat flour in this preparation. Add the cardamom powder and mix well.

Step 3: Add 2 teaspoons of Ghee (don't use all of it at once) and mix well into the flour such that it resembles bread crumbs. Hold the flour in your palm and press with your fingers. If the flour holds shape, you do not need to add any more ghee. If it does not, add some more a little at a time and check. Once it holds shape, move on to the next step.

Step 4: Add the sugar water little by little (do not add all of it at once) and knead a semi stiff dough.

Step 5: Next take a portion of the dough, roll into a thick disc (1/4 " in thickness and about 5" in diameter) and cut in into 4 equal parts running a knife or pizza cutter vertically and horizontally giving you 4 triangles. Here is where it gets the name Chothe (coming from the sindhi number 4). You could also use a cookie cutter to get a round even shape (the words Rot or Tikki come from the round shape) or any other cookie cutter for different shapes. Make small slits so that the pieces cook completely from the inside too when frying.

Step 6: Heat oil in a pan. When adding these Chothe, reduce the flame to low and fry until both sides turn a nice golden brown.

Optionally sprinkle some powdered sugar on the top, cool and serve. I also sprinkle dry edible rose petals for extra flavor and fragrance!

SINDHI VARO
(Dry Fruit Brittle)

Sindhi Varo is a traditional festive sweet made on the occasion of Diwali. I remember that while many of the other sweets we received as Diwali gifts, this one was always made at home.

The Sindhis have taken this dish a notch higher! It is made entirely from dry fruit and pistachios occupy a special place.

Taking on the tradition, I make this every Diwali to share with my friends and family.

213

Sindhi Varo

20 MINS   15 PIECES   EASY

INGREDIENTS

Dry Fruit (Chopped Almonds, Pistachios and Cashews) – 1 cup

Poppy Seeds – 1 tbsp

Dry Coconut – a few pieces

Cardamom Powder – ¼ tsp

(Mix these and keep ready in a single bowl)

Ghee – 1 tbsp

Sugar – 1 cup

Step 1: In a heavy bottomed pan, melt ghee and immediately add the sugar. Start caramelizing the sugar on low flame.

Step 2: When the sugar has completed melted, add the bowl of dry fruit, poppy seeds, dry coconut and cardamom powder. The next steps are done almost immediately so keep everything ready.

Step 3: Now pour this mixture on a greased surface and using a rolling pin (which is greased well) in a single direction, spread the mixture. Now you can use a knife or pizza cutter, and define the shapes lightly. Let the mixture cool completely.

Step 4: Once the mixture cools, it will harden and automatically come out of the greased surface. You can then break the brittle into smaller pieces or if you have lightly defined them in step 3, the brittle will break along those lines.

Make Varo this Diwali! Or serve it as dessert after meals or as a snack.

Bonus

Here are some more ideas...Besides the Garam Masalo, the rest are some quick meals that my mother made with whatever was available. Make these especially for the little ones in your family!

Garam Masalo

INGREDIENTS

Cumin Seeds (Jeera Seeds) – 75 gms

Black Pepper Corns – 15 gms

Cinammon Stick – 10 gms

Cloves – 7 gms

Green Cardamom – 2.5 gms

Black Cardamom – 5 gms

Nutmeg – 1/2

Bay Leaves – 7 gms

We do not use too many spices in our food. Occasionally there's the Garam Masalo that we like to sprinkle over some of the recipes, especially the non-vegetarian ones.

So, here's the traditional Sindhi Garam Masalo recipe. The unique point about this recipe is that it is mostly cumin seed based and does not use coriander seeds. In addition, it uses very few spices, yet is very flavorful and stirs magic into the simplest of recipes…

Step 1: In a heavy bottomed pan, dry roast the cumin seeds on low flame, for about 1 to 2 minutes until they turn aromatic and slightly dark. Take them out in a bowl.

Step 2: In the same pan, dry roast the rest of the spices except the bay leaves, for about 1 to 2 minutes. Take them out in a different bowl.

Step 3: Lastly, dry roast the bay leaves for about 30 to 40 seconds.

Step 4: Let all the spices cool completely. First, blend the bay leaves and cumin seeds to a fine powder. Next blend the rest of the spices. Mix well and your Garam Masalo is ready!

Biscuit Butter

This was a go-to snack whenever we were in a hurry. 'Invented' by my mom, it was my best friend's favorite! And mine too. When everyone else was making Bread-n-Butter, Mom would make us Biscuit-n-Butter. Her answer to all the cream/chocolate centered biscuits that were a new fad at the time and oh so expensive!

The melted butter trickling out of the tiny holes in the biscuits made them look so yummy and desirable! My son loves these too and the recipe passes on.

It was just Amul butter between two Marie biscuits (cookies) but boy, did they taste divine! Try this simple and easy snack!

Kheer Chanwar

(MILK AND RICE)

INGREDIENTS

Cooked Rice – ½ cup

Warm Milk – ½ cup

Sugar – 2 tsps

Cardamom Powder and other garnish – optional

I remember that my mom would be the last to eat in our household. Only after she had served all of us would she sit down for her meal. Sometimes, there would not be much left for her, because her food was always so tasty…At those times, she would take a small steel bowl, add the cooked rice, heat up some milk and pour it on top, stir in a little sugar and her meal – Kheer Chanwar – would be ready.

As she would sit to eat that, sometimes she would give the three of us a spoon or two and we would wonder how everything she touched turned so yummy!

Step 1: In a bowl take the cooked rice, pour warm milk over it and stir in the sugar. You could adjust the quantity of milk depending on the desired consistency.

Step 2: Garnish this humble dish with cardamom powder, almond slivers and saffron.

Serve Kheer Chanwar whenever you have leftover cooked rice!

Taryal Patata ain Mungphali

(FRIED POTATOES AND PEANUTS)

INGREDIENTS

Potatoes – 2 small

Raw Peanuts – ½ cup

Salt – as per taste

Pepper Powder – ¼ tsp

Mondays would be a day of fasting for my mom and she would combine fried potato wedges and fried peanuts to make the perfect combination for a fasting day.

Sprinkled with salt and pepper only, this is a very easy fasting meal.

Step 1: Chop the potatoes into wedges. You can keep the skin of the potatoes on.

Step 2: Deep fry in medium oil. Drain onto a kitchen towel when the wedges turn a light brown. Sprinkle salt and pepper powder.

Step 3: In the same oil, deep-fry the raw peanuts until they turn dark brown. Drain on kitchen towel and sprinkle some salt.

Serve this warm as a fasting meal or even as a snack!

Pohan jo Chivdo

(PUFFED RICE SAVORY SNACK)

INGREDIENTS

Poha (Puffed Rice - thick variety) – 1 cup

Raw Peanuts – ¼ cup

Salt – ½ tsp

Chili Powder – ½ tsp

Sugar – ¼ tsp

Oil – to deep fry

This snack is liked by everyone and is made in so many different ways especially during festivals like Diwali. The simplest version of this snack was made by my mom many times and not just during the festive season.

In its most basic form with just Poha (puffed rice) and peanuts, this snack tasted simply divine. That something available in the stores could be so conveniently made at home was a big revelation for the three of us and we would love to dig into the big steel container (dabbo) in which my mom stored this yummy treat.

Step 1: In a heavy bottom pan, on high flame, heat oil. When it is hot, lower the flame to medium and add the Poha, which will immediately rise up. Take the Poha out and drain on a kitchen towel.

(Note - Poha rises immediately in hot oil so ensure that there is enough space in the pan for the Poha to rise. Additionally pour only so much oil such that it does not spill over at the time.)

Step 2: In the oil, on medium flame, fry the peanuts. Remove and drain them on a kitchen towel when they have turned brown.

Step 3: Mix the Poha and the peanuts; add salt, sugar and chili powder. Serve when it has cooled to room temperature.

Bheendi Patata

(OKRA AND POTATOES)

INGREDIENTS

Okra – 10 to 15 (chopped into small pieces)

Potatoes – 1 medium sized (peeled and chopped into cubes)

Oil – 1½ tbsp

Turmeric Powder – ¼ tsp

Coriander Powder – ½ tsp

Mango Powder – ¼ tsp

Salt – as per taste

This recipe of Bheendi Patata is the fried version. There's no stuffing, no onions or tomatoes. Just dry spices but the recipe turns out as a great side to your main meal.

Try this one when you are low on time and other ingredients to make a curry. My mother made this recipe with other vegetables too – Eggplant, Bell Pepper and Cauliflower. It tastes great and is ready in no time. I also remember that she would pack this often in my father's lunch box.

Step 1: In a heavy bottom pan, on medium flame, heat oil. When the oil is hot, lightly fry the potatoes. Then add the okra pieces and fry the potatoes and okra together for 5 – 7 minutes. Keep stirring.

Step 2: Add all the dry spices including salt and fry the vegetables. Cover and fry alternately until the vegetables are cooked completely.

Serve warm at meal time with Phulko or Dal and Chanwar.

Suran Tuk

(ELEPHANT YAM FRY)

INGREDIENTS

Yam (peeled and chopped into pieces) – 2 cups

Coriander Powder – ½ tsp

Cumin Powder – ½ tsp

Red Chili Powder – ½ tsp

Mango Powder – ½ tsp

Salt – as per taste

Oil – to fry

Water to boil

Suran (Yam) Tuk is a delicious side with your regular meal. Simple and yet delightful.

Step 1: In a pressure cooker, cook the yam with water and salt. Switch off the flame after one whistle and open the lid of the pressure cooker once it depressurizes naturally.

Step 2: Drain the cooked pieces of yam on a kitchen towel and ensure the pieces are dry.

Step 3: In a heavy bottomed pan, heat oil on high flame and deep-fry the pieces of yam until they are crispy.

Step 4: Drain them; lightly press the pieces between your palms. Sprinkle salt and all the spices – cumin, coriander, red chili and mango powders.

Serve warm as your delicious crunchy side!

As you come to the end of this book, I hope that you have found recipes that perhaps you had forgotten, some that took you down memory lane, some that brought a smile to your face and some that you will make for your loved ones…

I am grateful that through my book, I was able to share my memories, my stories and my happiest moments. Thank you for providing me with this platform and for helping me keep the Sindhi cuisine alive in your hearts and in your kitchens!

www.ingramcontent.com/pod-product-compliance
Lightning Source LLC
Chambersburg PA
CBHW040258100426
42811CB00011B/1302